GABRIELLA MARIA BARNER

The Getaway

From a teen perspective

Contents

Foreword

The Get Away || From a teen perspective

"To all the parents, teachers, coaches, aunts, uncles, and adults all around the world, this may come as a surprise to you, but teens do have something to say. And if you open your mind and heart, you will be pleasantly and wonderfully surprised.

The teens of today are probably the most informed teens in the history of this modern world. Why shouldn't we be? We have social media, smart TVs, Alexa, Google, YouTube, Twitter, Instagram, and many more communications that put the world at our fingertips.

The Bible says in Joel 2:28, And it shall come to pass afterward that I will pour out My Spirit upon all flesh; and your sons and your daughters shall prophesy, your old men shall dream dreams, your young men shall see visions. "

~ Gabriella Maria Barner, Author of "The Getaway", Entrepreneur, & Speaker.

"I recently received a call from a very dear friend of many years requesting me to contribute to the foreword of his amazing daughter Gabriella Maria Barner new book, "The Getaway". I quickly asked, what daughter? Ms. Gabby... which I fondly call her. Absolutely I said, I would love too! As an author of several books, I know the hard work and patience that it takes for most authors to write a book. And to hear that Ms. Gabby has authored her first at the young age of 15 years is fantastic. She has masterfully written a book that speaks directly to parents about what teens and young adults are thinking about every day.

The daily news has one report after another about teens behaving badly, yet there are also teens who are encouraging and inspiring their peers to not only behave well and yet again, there are some teens who are influencing their peers to become leaders and world changers. I am excited to share one of those world changes with you in this book. Gabriella M. Barner is a young lady on a mission to help her peers and other young people to become all they can be. Many years ago I worked in the school system as a drug prevention coordinator, and we found that some of the most impactful influencers on teens were other teens who could influence their peers to behave and perform positively rather than negatively! I think this is a great example of that kind of peer influence and I believe that you will agree once you see the impact this book has on your teen. Gabrilella, or Gabby for short, is talking to teens in a way that they can not only hear her but also receive the information so they can be positively influenced! As an author of several best selling books, I know the hard work and patience that it takes to write a book. Gabby has written a book that speaks powerfully to teens and young adults to help them have greater success. In her book the Getaway, she has demonstrated a wonderful gift of being able to open up her heart and share things from that secret place that most teens dare not share. The Getaway, also encourages other teens and young adults to begin to communicate with their parents and enjoy the future that is ahead of them. I highly recommend you not only get a copy of this book for your teen but also for their friends, because we all know that who you hang around is who you will become like. So, if you want to have successful children you don't just want to influence them, but also influence those who they associate with on a daily basis. If you do, you will see this book not only as a resource more than just a book and the money you spend will become an investment rather than a cost. And in time you will be glad you made the investment."

~ **Dr. Willie Jolley, Hall of Fame Speaker, Nationally Syndicated Radio Show Host and Best Selling Author of A Setback Is A Setup For A**

Comeback and An Attitude of Excellence.

"I am so thrilled to have this opportunity to write a portion of the foreword of Gabriella Maria Barner's new book "The Getaway". To be asked by my friend from the east coast, Brother in Christ, and business partner, Dr. Honney (HL) Lavern Barner, is truly a blessing. Early this year I had the distinct pleasure of hosting the first "East Coast…West Coast high school zoom connection session for young teens in response to COVID 19. The goal was to gather their thoughts about the impacts of COVID 19 on their lives. Gabriella was one those high school teens on the zoom. I recognized from her responses that she was definitely in tune with what was going on in the world and was not going to let it stop her. Professionally, I engage young adults around the world but after reading "The Getaway" I have increased my knowledge and insights to young adults a hundredfold. If you want to know and understand what our teens and young adults are thinking simply read "The Getaway". I was particularly drawn to Chapter 3 "Social Media Woes" and Chapter 5 "Growing with God". I have been schooled by a teen. I know GREATNESS when I see it. Gabriella's greatness emanates from the words she's assembled throughout the pages of this soon to be Amazon #1 BEST SELLER!"

~ **Kevin Bracey, former Professional Baseball Player (Canada), Motivational Entertainer, Author of the book, "Scared Great".**

Preface

Gabriella M. Barner is an amazing, talented young school teen who is capturing the world by her grace, warm heart, intelligence, and beauty. She shares with her family and friends about the everyday struggle that teens and young adults go through. Her favorite expression is "Teens are People Too." She is absolutely correct. They are people too and the people that we must listen and include in our conversation because they are leaders of tomorrow.

Teens and young adults are the most valuable resources in our families, communities, cities, states, and this country we call America. This is not only unique to America but it is the same for every country on this earth. The United States is powerful due to two things; we honor God and the children He has entrusted us to love, raise and honor Him.

Gabriella invite you to take a short journey in "The Getaway" to get a glimpse at just a few things that teens are experiencing and thinking about today as they deal with life twist and turns, ups and downs, expectations, family, social media, maturing, and faith.

Acknowledgement

I acknowledge Jesus Christ as my Lord and Savior.

Thanks to my Dad Dr. Honney Lavern Barner and my Mom Franchestee J. Barner for having faith in me.

Thanks to my big brother, First Lieutenant Haven L. Barner, for his continued support and encouragement.

And to all my uncles, aunts, and cousins—there are many. I must also give a special shout out to my three close cousins: Cassidy, Jonathan, and Faith.

Finally, hello and thank you to all my friends at church, school, and in my local community.

Dedication

To all teens, high school students, college students, and young adults who have something to say but are not being heard.

To every teenager and young adult who is developing their relationship with God.

To every teenager and young adult who doesn't know Jesus Christ as their Lord and Savior.

To every parent with a teenager or young adult who encourages their children to speak.

To anyone who desires to share their thoughts with others.

To all my mentors who have poured into me over the years.

About the Author

Gabriella M. Barner is a bright, ambitious, and talented young girl growing in a very small town in Virginia. She's your typical high school student who is at the beginning of this amazing experience.

She enjoys music, gymnastics, dance, cheerleading, running track and playing the violin. She's a member of her high school track team, the cheer team and the Historian of her class. Believe it or not, she's a student cadet in the Junior Marine Corp ROTC program. She is also a member of the Wahoo Summer League Swim Team and the former Vice President of the Prince William NAACP Youth Council.

She has a long list of things that interest her, but I need not list them because by the time you read this book, she probably won't be interested in them anymore!

And to give you an idea of where she is in her life journey, she recently celebrated her 15th birthday celebrating Quinceanera style.

Prologue

Parents, if you want to know what we talk about, all you have to do is to either listen to your teen or read this book. I am a teen simply offering some words of encouragement, inspiration, guidance, opinions, and ideas. These are the things that we as teens share with each other because sometimes we don't think you hear us or believe us.

This is not a book that will identify all the woes and challenges that teens face every day. Nor will it complain about parents, teachers, coaches, and the like. Teens do profess to be experts or a know-it-all generation who merely want to be heard because we're fed so much information through social media, smart TVs, YouTube, Google, Facebook, Twitter, Instagram, and so much more—and then you expect us to be quiet and not get engage with the world around us.

We understand the "tradition" that children are to be seen and not heard. Respectfully, we are not growing up in the same way that our parents or grandparents did. We are constantly exposed to so much information without your guidance or explanation. Do you expect us to hear, read, and experience this fast-paced life driven by the information highway and not say anything?

Our acquisition of knowledge is growing rapidly during this social media age. We're not teens just from our local community, because you have expanded our community from being local to global. Our society is a global environment and we need to be heard so we can remind you we are teens.

We communicate with each other practically every minute of the day, seven days a week. There's a lot of information that's constantly flooding our minds, and a large amount of it is very negative and discouraging. Teens can be really bad at times. They say very mean things and then tell the rest of world. How can we focus on our schoolwork and other activities when we're focused on pleasing all the haters, bullies, and selfish teens we have to deal with every single day? If our parents don't talk to us someone else will and they will not have our best interest at heart. Hey Mom! Hey, Dad! Do you have a minute for me? I'm changing right before your eyes. Do you see me?

Chapter 1

Changes in my appearance

Hey you, yeah you, let's dive right in. If you didn't know already that your appearance is going to change, well, now you know. Everyone is not going to look the same. We're all made differently in our own way. We all have our pros and cons. We all have our own talents in different ways. As you grow up and mature through elementary, middle, and high school, your appearance will change; it's a part of life. You will have some insecurities, and that's normal. You are normal, even if you may not like the way you look. You are your own person; no one else in this world will look like you. Each person is different.

As we all grow up you will start too notice your weight shift up and down; you will see a change in your weight, curves, fat, and even muscle as the years go on. You might grow faster than your other friends, and you might feel the odd one out when you do. You may ask yourself, "Oh, why don't I look like them?" or "Why do I weigh more than her?" Remember, you're always going to be okay and be just as beautiful as them. Don't worry. We've all been there at least once with our friends. Don't worry about what people say and don't let them get to you.

Everyone goes through phases in life, even those who talk about you. Yes, they have their bad days also. One of the worst things to do while changing is to compare yourself with others. Comparing yourself to others will not help you at all. Comparing yourself will push you back from accepting your body instead of going forward and embracing yourself. While we all are going through changes in our appearance, embrace what you love about yourself. Pick out the things you love about yourself and focus on those things, not on the things you don't like. Start with the positive and quit with the negativity. If you pick out the things you love about yourself, you could help someone else out.

Someone could look up to you, and you could be a role model to others and you may not even know it. If someone looks up to you and notices that you're insecure about the way you look, it's not helping them or you. If those people who look up to you see that you're struggling, they might go back to their old ways and start picking out their weakest points in themselves. As soon as you bring yourself down, people can tell; those influencers can read your mind. As soon as you bring yourself up, they will begin to bring themselves up.

So let me tell you a quick story. One day other girls were bullying a girl named Victoria about her appearance. Victoria is a volleyball player for her school. She had overheard what they were saying about her. Their names were Ashley and Kelly, and they would not stop talking about how fat Victoria looked. A couple of days went by and Victoria was starting to feel insecure and self-conscious. She started feeling ashamed of her body. A week later she had a game for her school and she didn't want to wear her uniform because she thought people could see that she was fat. She hated wearing her uniform. The next day at school Ashley and Kelly were giving her bad looks, and posted something on social media about her. It got to Victoria so bad that she wanted to quit playing for her school. One day they had a team sleepover and her teammates picked her back up. They played music as she sat by the bonfire with her teammates. Victoria was surrounded by people who showed her love, and to let her know that we all have things that we don't like about ourselves but that you shouldn't let people walk all over you. Surround yourself with positive people and don't worry about the negative.

The next day Ashley and Kelly still wanted to get into Victoria's head about how she looked. Once they were all in class together Victoria turned around and said to them, "People will always have their opinions of you even if they know how successful you will be one day." Then, later that day, Ashley and Kelly didn't have a word to say to Victoria and to anyone else.

People will always judge you and you won't always like it. If you feel that you're getting heavy you can do things that make you feel happy: go on a run, go on a hike, work out, cook, play games, paint, or even do yoga. Finding something you love to do is important. Taking time for you is very important. Self care, and self-love can play a big role in where you start, and where you stay.

One day my Dad told me a story about a young girl. She was short and she enjoyed playing softball. Her team tryouts were coming up and she started to get excited. Her family was supportive and encouraged her to try out. She started to get nervous as the tryout date was coming up and she wanted to bail out. Then her family gave her some encouraging words. This was the week before tryouts and she was on the edge of her seat. She later convinced her friend to try out as well. She was looking forward to hopefully being on the team with her friend. The week of tryouts was finally here, and all she could think about was tryouts. One morning she was in the cafeteria at school. She was waiting for her friend in line to get her food. Then, as she was getting ready to leave, some girls found out that she was going to try out for softball. They were giving her looks and laughing at her. Later on that day she saw the girls that were making fun of her for trying out. She started to feel bad about herself and started to feel down. After the first day of tryouts, she and her friend went back into the locker room to change to go home. The only thing she could think about was how the girls were talking about her.

When she returned home, her older sister asked her what was wrong. She told her what happened and her sister gave her a hug and talked all night with her. On the second day she was back out on the field working hard to prove to those girls that they shouldn't be talking about her in the first place. The girls told her that she was too short to play, she wasn't good at all, and that she wouldn't make any team. She ran home and told her sister what they said to her. Her sister kept on pushing her younger sister, and told her that there's a height requirement to play softball. You don't have to have huge hands to play, and your weight doesn't have anything to do with it either. Then, this was the last day of tryouts and this was going to be a banger! This is the final and last day the girls would find out if they made the team or not.

After school was over, she told herself that she was going to make the team regardless of what others said about her. After the third day, each of them were called in one by one. This was the moment! She had tons of butterflies in her stomach, and her friend told her she was going to be okay and to go in with her head up high. She walked out of the room running straight to her friend and told her that she made the team. They couldn't stop jumping for joy that they both had made the team together. Words of encouragement from her family and friends had helped her so much throughout the week. She called her sister and told her that she made a team and then called her family. They told her they always knew that she could do it.

You can do anything you put your mind to even though things will take time and effort; nothing comes easy. Patience, endurance, dedication are required. After her four years of high school she kept putting all her energy into softball. Her senior year was coming up and she was very much excited for it. She was the captain of her team, and was still working hard to play for college. Day in and day out she was out on the field or training with her older sister. She was determined to play for college; she knew that this ride wasn't over yet. She thanked God for every moment. Then she started to get recruited by colleges one after another. During the spring she committed to the University of Florida. She decided that she was not done yet with her career. The summer

4

before going to Florida she was excited to play and meet her new roommate. They started training and her goal was to be the best of the best.

She was given awards after awards; she started her own training camps to inspire other girls that wanted to play for college and proved to be an inspiration to many. She thanked the people who bullied her because, with the support of friends and family, it pushed her into becoming the person she was today. She let no one drag her down, and prayed and thanked God every day for the opportunities that she had.

We've all heard this but it's true: "Don't judge a book by its cover." What you see on the outside is not always what's on the inside. My Mom told me that when she was in high school there was this girl who everyone talked about: that she was so pretty, all the guys wanted to date her, she always had the latest trending clothes, had tons of money, and was a cheerleader for her school. She had a boyfriend who was a student athlete as well. Everyone wanted to be friends with her and everyone talked about her. She had it all; she had the best parents, and she was super fun to be around. Her parents were so welcoming to everyone, and filled everyone with joy. She would have parties for holidays at her house. She truly loved life. She didn't have to worry about having dinner that night, having clothes on her back, shoes to wear, money to spend, or a car to drive. Everyone described her as having a perfect life.

About ten years later someone from her class was walking around downtown and saw a woman who appeared to be in a bad way. This person was going out to eat with their family, and then they stopped and went up to this woman and asked her what her name was. She told the man her name, and his response was that she was in his graduating class. He had asked her what happened? Why was she living on the streets? Yes, she was homeless. She had no money and nowhere to stay. He was completely shocked. So many people thought she had everything—and was rich, so why would this happen to her? She's a perfect example of not judging a book by its cover; you never know what people are like on the inside. She may have been going through some rough times at home or school. So what you see on the outside may not be what you think they are on the inside.

If your friends are feeling down about something, cheer them up! Show them that they are loved, and that they don't need to look like or be anyone else. Trying to change yourself into something you're not can be a big mistake; it is never the answer. You don't need to look or act like someone else. Being you is you; you are enough! Don't let others tell you how to live. Having people to look up to you is good. At the same time, people can be so insecure and you can help them by doing simple things. Tell them a positive quote, show them a photo or letter can mean a lot to someone who's feeling crappy. When you're at school, go sit with someone who you don't usually sit with or would talk to. If they seem lonely or sad, try to cheer them up, and learn something new about them. You can also help someone out outside of school. We all love Chick-fil-A, so you could do something as simple as paying for the people behind you. Paying for someone's meal could help a person out and put a smile on their face. You have no clue what that person or family is going through. They could be going from meal to meal, and decided they wanted Chick-fil-A that day. Always try to do something nice for other people!

Chapter 2

Getting closer to adulthood

Whoa, that word: "adulthood." Anxious? Well, every day we're getting closer to growing up, going to college, graduating from college, to getting a place by yourself. You have to learn how to pay the bills, wash dishes, do your laundry, cook, clean, and more. After graduating some go into the military, college, or they go out and try to find a job. My cousin told me that she's excited for a new chapter but also nervous and doesn't want to leave home. She's use to staying home, and she grew up her whole life in one spot. She's nervous about going out into the real world, with many people. She doesn't want to leave her family and friends; but she's excited for a new chapter. One major thing in growing older is taking responsibility for your actions. Sometimes that may not be as easy as it sounds.

As we grow older we have different responsibilities, whether you decide to cook food for yourself, do chores around the house or apartment, go to class if you're in college, or others things. Making sure you get everything on your bucket list completed for the day is important. You're a student in college, so you want to make sure you get your work done on time, which includes taking time out to study. If you decide to sleep in for a class, you should take responsibility for sleeping in. If you forget to pay for your food, make sure you own up to your actions. As you can see, taking responsibility for your actions is important, especially as you grow closer to adulthood—and especially for those who are about to go off to college: You won't be able to rely on your parents for everything anymore.

You will have to start managing your money and learn how to pay for your food, gas, insurance, or phone bill. Free time is important but balancing it all can be hard and takes some time to get used to. As you grow older you discover that your free time becomes shorter and shorter. You have to work, find time to sleep, spend time with your family, and attend school/classes. Even if you don't want to, you will have to start learning how to multi-task and get things done on time. You will take your homework to work, write a paper while listening to an ebook, or wash clothes while studying for a test. You won't have much time so you will try doing two things at once. While this may make things a little easier be careful not to overwhelm yourself. To put this in blunt terms, you may have to choose between getting a new cell phone and making your next car insurance payment.

Paying for your needs isn't all fun, but that's life. Choosing your needs definitely isn't easy, but it will pay off in the long run. You just need to put forth the effort. Making sure that you know the difference between your needs and your wants is extremely important. Another thing: If you don't already know how to change a tire, check the oil in your car, or how to jump-start a car, you need to learn these skills. Breaking down on the side of the road and not knowing how to do simple things will be embarrassing, and when your tire is flat it's grounds for divorce in some states, so it's good to learn that sooner—LOL. Oh yeah, knowing how to do your taxes as a student would be good as well.

Also, if you don't already, learn how to swim! It's surprising how many people don't know how to swim. When you go to pool parties you don't want to be the only one to not know how. Also, knowing how to swim is actually an excellent skill to have because you never know when it could come in handy (fun fact: your body is already 60 percent water). Also, learn how to fix basic household problems like changing a light blub. Learn how to build a fire. I find it surprising that many don't know how to. It's a good basic thing to learn.

Learn to develop good communication skills. Learn how to talk to others, and take baby steps if you're shy and afraid to talk to others. One day when you're older, you will have a job, and more than likely you will have to give a presentation, or talk in front of a crowd. You want to be able to have confidence to talk to others and sound trustworthy. You want to talk clear, look people in the eye, and show them that you know what you're talking about. Show them that you're the person for the job and present yourself well. You don't want to sound untrustworthy or unknowledgeable.

Communicate through body language. Your body language can tell people everything they need to know before you even open your mouth. Don't break eye contact with the person you're having a conversation with. Giving them your full attention is important, even if you don't mean to come off as rude, or snobby. This can happen, and it's happened to me, where people think I'm being rude. I'm not. I'm giving you my full attention!

Now, for every conversation you don't need to have full eye contact. You don't want to seem like you're staring somebody down. You'll know the right time when to make eye contact. Developing this skill during young adulthood will help once you're off to go to college because you will find yourself being forced to get close to people.

I know you may be a bit frightened to meet new people, but it will be okay. You get to learn about many different backgrounds, religions, and cultures. You'll learn that you will have similarities and differences. You will meet some of your life-long friends in college and in the workforce, so learning to engage well with others is crucial.

And then there's money. Sticking to a budget, especially if you're in college, is important. It's interesting to me how many people don't know how to stay within a budget. I love to shop, and I'm very much obsessed, so I can see it may be hard not to spend tons of money. When balancing a checkbook, make sure there's more coming in than going out. Set aside money for emergencies and don't touch it unless you have a true emergency. Make sure that you don't tell anyone about where that money is; it's your safe money.

Also, growing a relationship between you and God should be a priority throughout your life along with building friendships. You will want to have fun and enjoy life to the absolute fullest and it is always good to share it with a close friend. God, family, and friends will be there with you, throughout all of it. Also learn to build your character in your teen years because a strong character will be with you forever. Decide what you want to be known for and cultivate that to the best that you can.

As you grow older, have strong values so that you can bring something to the table. Be yourself, and don't try to change yourself for others. At the end of the day you want to be joyful. You don't want to "fake it" and be unhappy with a personality that isn't real.

Make sure you want to leave on a good note, and you want people to remember your name for something great. Be different; try to be the one to stand out, in a good way. Build your character now as a teen and the result will be with you when you grow up. Learning how to negotiate with others is very important. You will have different opinions with people. It may be in a class or outside of class, and you will often have to negotiate with others. It should always be done in a respectful way. Everyone has different ways of how they see things. You want to do your best with getting your point across while still coming off as friendly. Stand your ground, and get your thoughts across. You can be persuasive, and you could maybe consider their thinking. Just know that you need to negotiate in a respectful and responsible way.

Another key is taking the initiative and not having to be told to do a task.

Doing this can be useful in many ways. For an example, take care of your needs before others have to tell you. If you're at work and your boss notices something that needs to be done, go ahead and do the task without anyone telling you to do it. It shows leadership and responsibility, and you will be setting an example for others to follow. You never know when you can impress others, and it could help you out at the same time. Learn to do things on your own, such as cleaning and cooking. Take care of your basic needs.

Using your time wisely is key, especially when you're in college or in the work force where you will need to learn time management. You're going to have a lot on your plate after high school. The ability to take advice and to listen more than you speak is a sign of a successful person. You can always be a silent leader, and show others how you can handle big tasks. Guide others, sit back, and just show actions. What the other person shared is valuable information, and you may be able to use it. If you need suggestions for a topic, have someone else do the talking. You can still make your point across and ask for what you want, while appearing reasonable and collaborative with the other person. Also, know to take full responsibly for your mistakes; own them, and then acknowledge your mistakes. We all make mistakes, but it's how to acknowledge your mistakes that matters. You will always make mistakes. Everyone does, even when they're older. Don't blame others for what you did. Don't complain. Talk about how you're going to be better the next time. If you did something wrong, apologize, and then be glad that you took that action.

Another key is to be able to take constructive feedback. There are two types of criticism: constructive and destructive. Constructive criticism is someone saying to you, "What could I do better?" We all can improve on something, so having people tell you where you could improve is always helpful. Constructive criticism answers the question how to be better. What does not help is destructive criticism, which is when someone points out all the tasks you do poorly and all your faults and weaknesses. Behaving this way can come off as highly disrespectful. It is hurting you more than helping you. It can result in someone developing insecurity and jealousy. It brings out the worst in some people. If you're not one who takes horrible criticism well, I would recommend growing thicker skin, so to speak, so that you won't be too upset at these times. As you grow older, someone may ask for help. If they want your help, make sure you know how much criticism they can take; everyone is different when they want feedback. Also make sure that you can take feedback as well.

Also stop making excuses, and when you're asked to do something, make sure you know what you're supposed to do—and do it. As an example if you had a meeting at 2:00 P.M. and arrived late, don't blame it on traffic. Be responsible, and say that you didn't leave exactly on time, like you planned. As much as blaming it on traffic sounds easier, just be straight up honest. Ask yourself next time, "What can I do now so this doesn't happen next time?" To not make the same mistake, set an alarm on your phone next time and get ready 30 minutes earlier, so you know that you will be ready. Know and understand what you promise others, as silly as that may sounds. I can also have trouble with keeping promises, but I like to think they're little promises, never something important! I have in mind little things such as promising someone you will bring them a pencil or a charger. If you do promise something, do your best to follow through with it. Someone who holds to their word will be perceived as a person of their word. You will know that you can always count on that person for anything. If something does pop up, talk to that person, and explain to them that you're unable to keep that promise except, of course, if something serious comes up. Be a realist and only say that you'll do something if you truly believe that you're able to keep your promise.

There are many things that you can learn as you grow and get closer to adulthood. Knowing what you want in life is a big part of growing up. Yes, it may be hard especially living as a teen and you want to enjoy life. But growing up will come around very soon; it seems far away, but in reality, time will fly by like a blink of an eye. Taking action, once you know what you want in life, can bring you closer to your goal. When things go wrong, don't doubt yourself. There will be struggles or difficulties as you start on your journey. No one is perfect, and we all go through lows before we get to our highs. Be grateful through the process, and thank God that you're able to live your life and go through lows, and highs, which will shape you into the person you want to become when you're older. Go through the storms. Yes, sometimes you will feel like you want to give up, but imagine where you will be at the end of your goal. If you quit, you won't ever get to see where you could go and become. I've had times where I felt like quitting, but then I persevered and got done what I needed to do. Be grateful that you're able to have goals.

Some may never know what they want to be. Some teens and young kids maybe never get to grow older and have their dreams come true. Be grateful for everything you have, including all the chapters in your life. You are living through chapters, and then when you get older, you will have finished writing your book. You will look back at your life and remember all the chapters that you went through. Be grateful for all the lessons you will get, some may never even get to have an education, some may never be able to have a job, some may never own a house. So be grateful that you can live your life to the fullest. Love the challenges, even though they are rough, be grateful. Know that you are blessed to have choices—and to be an adult and to be successful.

Lastly, and more important is learning how to take care of yourself. Make sure that you are happy, and find something that you can always do to uplift your mood. With all the seriousness I talked about throughout this chapter, just make sure that the "chapters" in your life are worth reading. If you have negative thoughts, then you will have negative experiences. When you have positive thoughts, you will have positive experiences. Enjoy your teen years while you don't have to pay any bills!

Chapter 3

Social Media Woes

Social media. Let's talk about it. How do you look at the media? Do you look at it as positive, negative, or both? I think it could be both, because I've seen many situations where it can be positive or negative. It should be used more for positivity; these days tons of people have a habit of bringing other people down. You could use it to talk to your friends, especially if they live far away. If you have family members who live in different countries, they're a call away. Some families live thousands of miles away, and can't see each other for a while. Some only see them once or twice a year and social media can be handy in this case. You can go live on Instagram, and answer questions that your friends and family ask you. If you have a dad, mom, brother, sister, aunt, or uncle in the military and they are deployed, you could post on Instagram or Snapchat and they can see what you're up to. As everyone can see, it's also used for advertising cars, food, diapers for babies, etc.

Advertising is big on Instagram and Snapchat. Both services can see what you follow and suggests ads you may be interested in: drawing the audience in, trying to sell their product, and then maybe getting people to buy their product. They see what you like to see and do, who you follow—and then ads start coming in. They suggest accounts and items you should look into, so it could be good if you own a business. If you own or work for a business it could be good for advertising.

Another pro is keeping up to date with the latest trends. Following people who are trendy could help you stay up with the latest. It could be a faster way of getting information out. Social media is helpful for fundraisers, pop-up shops, toy drives, food drives, and garage sales. If you want to put information out to buy your book, or anything else out, an ad on social media can get to people much faster. You can share, use hash tags, tag people in pictures, and go live as well. There are many ways that social media can provide positive aspects.

But there are always ways that social media can be used in a negative way. People start using it as a way to get to someone; this can go very badly for some people. Human trafficking is also big when people put their location on post and cause many things to go badly from there. Although Snapchat is cool too have, you need to know there could be some things that you should look out for. Having your location turned on in Snapchat could hurt you as well and you may not know it. Knowing that you should be careful when you accept an add-on is important. If you post a picture on Instagram and you are young, pretty, and people know you, predators may try to track you down.

Human trafficking is easily used with Instagram. It's shocking to realize that young children, adults, and especially teens are still getting kidnapped. Many teens still don't know what can happen and what the impact can be on using all social media. Predators can make fake accounts, follow you, and even start to track where your friends are. They could find out what state you live in, what school you attend, and you wouldn't even know.

Many teens don't pay attention to what they're doing or how they're behaving. For example, social media can be used for bullying. What you say behind a screen is different from what you would say in person. People know how to talk so angrily behind a screen, and then when they get in front of you they seem all friendly with you. Some people get torn down so much that they become sad, depressed, and have no one to talk to. They get judged for acting different and then the next day you may hear they committed suicide and it was because people were talking badly about them.

One time I was walking in the hallway, and this boy was looking down; he looked like he was crying. I walked up and asked him what was wrong, and he told me people were bullying him online and he didn't know what to do. He was very sad and seemed to be overwhelmed. Then the next day he wasn't at school, and it went on for about a week. Then he showed up to school and told me he wasn't doing well, so I prayed on it and then eventually he was better even though it didn't come easy. People don't know how much words can impact someone's life.

You may think it's all fun and games, but each person can take things differently. One person thinks it's a joke until something happens to that person and you can't take anything back. Once a comment is "out there" it's out there and hard to take back. What you say about someone can hurt. It's never fun to be on the other side of the phone. Remember, actions speak louder than words. People sometimes don't know what a person is going through and so putting someone down doesn't help matters. Putting people down is terrible thing to do and should not be done. No good can ever come from it. It's not worth it.

Did you ever see the movie *Central Intelligence* starring Dwayne Johnson? This was such a good movie. Johnson played the part of a fat high school kid named Bob Stone. Bob was picked on and bullied by others in his class. They played tricks on him and called him names. He was thought of as the fat person who would not succeed in life. They told him he would never have a girlfriend or get married. Because his classmates treated Bob so horribly he was always depressed. However, 20 years later Bob came back to a class reunion and no one recognized him, not even his best friend (Calvin Joyner) from high school. He was tall and looked like a bodybuilder. He was extremely handsome. They could not believe that it was Bob Stone from high school. He had drastically changed to a totally different person. This is an example of how not to judge a book by its cover. What I mean by this is you should treat everybody how you want to be treated because we're all humans and we're all a work in progress. As you can see from Bob Stone, he may have been a kid in high school with few friends because he was fat and out of shape. He grew up to be a successful and handsome young man that any woman would want to be with. At the high school reunion all of the people who made fun of him wanted to be his friend. They were all wishing they had treated him better in high school. You see, they didn't realize Bob was going to turn out to be such a popular guy.

Another story is that there was this little girl who was adopted but not many other people knew. As she got older she was interested in adoption and knew what it was about. These people at her school always had something to say about it. They thought she was weird and annoying. One day on social media they made a page on Instagram called "fun and games" but to some people it wasn't. One day she saw what they said about adoption, and she thought it was about her. All week she had to go to school with these groups of people, and they just stared and laughed at her. They would all still post pictures and make fun of other people as well. Then she confronted them about it. They didn't care and the teacher didn't do anything about it either. The teacher told her that she couldn't do anything about it because it wasn't her problem. She would go home and cry all the time because they wouldn't stop. The bullying would be more outside; it started to become a problem at school. All of them would throw pencils at her and call her names. She felt so horrible walking into school and having class with them. She went up to them and asked nicely to stop posting pictures about her. They wouldn't listen to her, but then little did they know that the girl didn't show up for a week. They were wondering where she went, why she wasn't at school. Then the student teacher heard and asked them "Why do you all care so much? You guys always bullied her." Little did they know she was diagnosed with stage 3 cancer, and she died that same week. Then it hit them, and then they realized they made her feel even worse. They made her sad all the time. No one knew what was wrong with her. People were making jokes, but they didn't know what she was going through. So then they started to care, and they took a step back. They can't even say sorry to the girl because she is gone. You don't know what another person is going through outside of school until something happens. If these kids didn't make an Instagram page, and had not bullied her, she could feel that she was worthy and had something going for herself. Since they made this page she gave up her fight. She didn't see there was a purpose in life anymore. She asked herself one day, "Why am I fighting anymore? No one cares about me anyway." Bullying doesn't make you cool, or fit in, or funny. It makes you stand out in a bad way. It's unfair and it doesn't make you bigger than others. Just imagine if you were on the other side going through cancer, and getting bullied while going to school everyday, for five days a week, for at least eight hours. Take a step back sometimes and check yourself and see what *you* are doing. Bullying people is never a good thing, and it brings people down.

Social media can be used for scamming, especially if you don't know what to look out for. Teens and the elderly tend to get scammed the most because often they don't pay attention. One scam for an example could be go to this location and get a free gift card to somewhere you like. Boom, there could be a hundred different things that could happen. You could get injured, hurt, in danger, anything. All because you didn't know what to look out for. Think about it: You don't know who these people are and who was on the other end of the screen. You could get kidnapped! The world is crazy and you don't know who to trust. Scammers can get your credit card and pull money out of your bank account. So knowing what to look out for is very important, especially on social media. Social media can also be such a distraction, especially to us teens. I'm going to be completely honest: There are some apps that I get distracted by that take up my time. I'm going to admit I could be on one app and then see myself still there two or three hours with my food and chilling. It can be nice sometimes to take a step back and chill;

we all could use that time. I love some days to do absolutely nothing and take a day off; we all should do that. Then I realize I need to get up and get my work done. At the same time you should know when to put your phone down and take a break. Maybe set a timer on your phone to know when to get on your school work, when to workout, to take the dog on a walk, to make lunch for your family. All that said, knowing your limit is important. Doing your work is more important than being on your phone. Phones in general can be super distracting, especially for teens and young adults. Some of us grew up on tablets and phones, and that's what we know to always go to. But make a decision to sometime to *not* pick up your phone and instead go on a walk or get some exercise. Pick something productive to do instead of scrolling through Snapchat and Instagram all day. Social media can take away from your schoolwork, and can take up a lot of your time in general. Scrolling through social media won't help you get your education, but hitting those books will, and studying will. Set a challenge for yourself, two or three times out of the week try to only look at your phone only for homework, work, and other needs. I know this could be hard for many, but try to go on a social media detox. Try to not go on social media for a week and see how much you can accomplish. I do that sometimes during my school year and it works like a gem.

I really find myself more productive, and I feel accomplished. I delete the app or unload the app for a week and don't touch it. If you try that you could really see yourself being productive. I've gotten so much stuff done, like doing all my homework, going on a run, focusing on myself. You could make up many challenges for yourself to better yourself. If you set small goals in your life as a teen, then imagine how far you will go when you get older. Don't get me wrong though, social media can be used in great ways as well. Just know how to use it and be mindful of your time. I use social media to talk to friends, ask questions, but I don't abuse it. So some days you need to shut social media off, and take a break, and go after those goals you would like to accomplish!

Chapter 4

New Interest

C hange is good; sometimes some may or may not like change. You can lose interest in things because you don't enjoy your activities, or want to do other things, such as other clubs or sports at school. Your hobbies, friends, work, school, and not just sports can all change overtime. Let's say you may like swimming, and you were on a competitive team and then all of a sudden you like football, and change into another sport. Sometimes you can lose interest in things you love and then you drift away from it. Sometimes this can make you sad or depressed. We have all those off days and are down, so you may not want to go to practice, or work out, or go to a meeting for a club you're involved in. That doesn't mean that it's for good, that you don't enjoy what you're doing. It could be your absolute favorite thing to do in the world and you want a break or a change of scenery to start enjoying other things. If people don't support your decisions, or you move on, don't think about them for a second. Take time for yourself and ask yourself "Am I really going to keep continuing the things that aren't in my best interest to make someone else feel happy?" "Am I going to live through their moments of happiness?" "Is it worth continuing what I'm doing, or moving forward, and growing in my new shell?" When you do move forward there will be days that you want to go back.

Growing up and moving on and looking back on your accomplishments feels good, because you knew at the end of the day that *you* did that, you won your happiness in that sport, club, or team. There are days that I wish I could go back to my old sports and do it all over again because it was exciting, interesting, dare-deviling, and so real! You learn so much through activities, you meet new people, travel, and grow mentally and physically.

Getting that feeling of "winning" and knowing that you accomplished your goals is such a good feeling. So yes, it's normal to look back and think about how much you enjoyed pushing yourself. Days in and out of practice and working hard with blood, sweat, and tears, days that you felt like giving up, are honestly the best days. Those are the days that you grow into the person you are. If you do activities other than sports, such as theater, doesn't it feel good to know that you nailed that play? Those that are in the band, doesn't it feel great to know that you all did your part and sounded like an ensemble? So yes, you will look back at the amazing moments that you made, and all the people you met throughout your activities.

If you have a goal and you haven't reached it, don't give up. If you're too scared for your dreams then you haven't reached your goals yet. What would you do if you weren't afraid? So if you have a dream to go pro, be a college athlete, go to the Olympics, be on a world team, be president, write a book, don't give up. If your dreams don't scare you, you haven't dreamed big enough. There will never be a dream that is too small.

If you feel like moving onto something else, don't move on because you don't think you can do it. Finish what you started. If your friend is leaving your team or club, don't leave because they are. Just because your friend is losing interest doesn't mean you are. Just because they decide to move on, and you know that you have a goal that you haven't reached yet, don't let that one person hold you back.

If your friend is leaving your sports team and tells you the next practice will be their last because they are moving on, that's great for them, but if you left it might not be so great for you. If you decide to leave, and think to yourself how you didn't even accomplish your dream, you will wish you could go back.

You don't ever have to follow others. Make sure you came there for what you wanted to do. Obstacles are the cost of greatness. Your journey may be a slow process, but quitting won't speed it up. On the other hand, if you want to move on because you feel accomplished, and want to move onto new adventures, that's great. There's always room for new interests, so go out and explore new things. Experiencing new adventures and obstacles are always new, fun, and rewarding. What you are into next will be challenging whether it may be another sport, becoming president of your club, joining the military, whatever. There will always be bumps and challenges on your journey.

God will lead you along the way. Again, you may feel like giving up, but you'll get through it. Believing in you even if others don't is key. Blocking out what others will say is also important. It will never be easy to move onto something else, especially if it's something different, but different can be great.

One time, my friend and I were going on a long walk near the ocean. We talked about school, sports, and friends, traveling together, mostly about anything that came to mind. We stopped by an ice cream store nearby. We were eating our ice cream while going on our walk. Maria ended up getting cookie dough, and I got french vanilla. Maria ended up getting toppings as well; they were falling right out her cone, and we just laughed. It felt like 120 degrees outside. Our ice cream was melting and dripping all over us. Then we stuffed it all in our faces before walking back to my house. Our mothers were sitting on my couch talking and noticed we were giggly. They both called us over and noticed our ice cream all over our hands. We all burst out laughing and headed to the beach.

We then saw some huge waves, and wanted to see if we could catch some. We hoped we could, so we packed some snacks and we hurried off. Then, we saw this huge shark, and we still wanted to go out. The lifeguard down at the beach told us it probably wouldn't be safe for us to go. We decided to just go to the pool instead, but we still would have had lots more fun catching some waves. We ended up talking about sports, as usual. We always kept up with the latest and greatest in sports. I asked Maria how swimming was going for her. We used to swim together, but not that day because I ended up getting something in my eye. She seemed like she didn't want to talk about it, so I let her have her space. We were both called in for dinner, and we were sitting together watching baseball for the rest of the evening.

About a week or two later, I asked Maria how swimming was going, and she told me she wanted to give it up. She told me she wanted to try something different. I was shocked, I thought sure she was going to keep doing it through college. We were both extremely excited when she was getting offers. I was talking to her about it, and I asked her "Why would you give up swimming now?" Maria was doing so great; I was thinking to myself why would she throw it away like that? I asked her what she wanted to do instead of swimming. So she told me she wanted to try CrossFit. So Maria decided that she wanted to try to do both, but only for a while. She only told me that she was going to do swimming for a little bit, but she would eventually quit. She knew that it was going to be a tough decision to make. She was so nervous to tell her parents, because she didn't want to disappoint them especially because of the money they both poured into swimming. I told her that I would always be here for her whether she was going to do both or none at all; she would always be my best friend. I would always be there by her side to support her decision. She was so thankful that I said that. Maria got to meet so many people through swimming, and she was very blessed that she was able to do the sport. She met Olympians, she went to swimming training camps, and started receiving offers for division one colleges, but then it all changed when a friend introduced her to CrossFit. She was hooked and wanted to try it one day, so she gave her friend a call on the phone. By the next week Maria was in the gym training with her friend, working hard, sweat dripping down her T-shirt, socks sweaty, and face red as a tomato. She was about to go on their mile run and her legs were on fire; she couldn't even walk after her friend's workout. The next day she told me she could barely walk. Surprisingly, she told me that she enjoyed it. So she signed up for classes to come back and start training with her friend. She was gaining muscle, and her parents didn't like the idea that she was doing CrossFit and taking away time from swimming. Maria's coach saw that she was extremely tired during morning practices, so he suggested that she shouldn't put in as many hours in the gym. As much as her parents and coaches told her that they didn't like her doing CrossFit, or as much, she still would go back. Maria and I were walking on the boardwalk one day, and she told me that she was going to tell her parents that she wanted to give up swimming because she really preferred CrossFit. I told her to go for it, and I would be there when she told her parents. As far as Maria is concerned, she loved the environment, and being with others trying to push others and break their personal records. She ended up competing more and more. Her parents still wish she didn't enjoy it as much as she did. There was always great competition around her.

She loved the idea that everyone was there for one goal, and it was to become better. They were all having the time of their lives, bloody hands, sweat rolling down their back, and tears of hard work and determination. She explained to her parents and coaches that she was happy and wanted to move forward with CrossFit. She wanted to compete around the country, and with other motivated individuals. They didn't like the idea at first because of all the years of hard work and money they had put into swimming. For her to quit was very troubling for them. Then after they saw her for the first time in the gym, training, and enjoying it, they started to come around. She was putting tons of hours in the gym, eating healthy, and making sure she got rest (recovering was all-important to her). Her family came out to her first competition against others, and unexpectedly she came in fifth place out of the 19 girls who competed. They started going to more competitions, and they finally started to support, and open up, and they saw her that she was happy and that she was doing what she enjoyed. Maria hit many obstacles along the way, even received a couple of injuries, but never too bad. Maria started to become one of the fittest teens on Earth; she was on many CrossFit channels. Maria still does CrossFit, and she doesn't take it back for one bit. She also encourages other teens, adults, and kids to do it as well. She thinks back on those days and the videos of her getting first place, breaking personal records, traveling, and meeting tons of people on the way. She thinks about the exciting moments when she swam. Most of it was more mental than physical because you have to believe in yourself before others do. So if you change over to a new interest, it can turn out for the better. Don't settle for less than what you want to do, and don't let others hold you back. Just because someone else decides to move on doesn't mean you have to as well. Accomplish those goals you set for yourself. Go on new adventures, be bold, and be brave.

Chapter 5

Growing with God

Do you know who God is? Do you know who your Lord and Savior is? Who is God? Do you want to learn more about Him? Let's start with this: He died on the cross for our sins, and rose on the third day to live on this beautiful Earth with us. He has a reason for everything. We may never understand His wisdom, but we will have to trust His actions. God has really helped me through so many rough times.

He is so powerful, and if you don't know Him, you should try to make an effort to grow a relationship with Him. He has done so much for us; so the least you could do is try to make an effort to call on His name by praying daily and reading His Word daily. If you don't know who He is and want to know more, you could go to a local church and join a local group. Trust me, you will never regret this decision. If you know Him and want to learn more, join a group, meet up at a coffee shop, and take notes, draw pictures to help you understand the word. You can always call on Him for anything.

One of my favorite scriptures is John 3:16: "For God so loved the world that He gave His only begotten Son, that whosoever believeth in Him shall not perish but have everlasting life." This verse to me says that God loves this world and loves us, and that we should believe in His son and whoever believes in Him will have eternal life in Heaven. Another scripture I like is Philippians 4:13: "I can do everything through him who gives me strength." I believe that I can do everything and anything through Him. It's not about your dreams; it's about how you're going to get there, and that's through him. He will give me and you strength to do anything.

When I used to have a big test coming up, or when I had a gymnastics competition, I would write Philippians 4:13 on my stomach with a black sharpie, and then when I felt butterflies I would rub my stomach. I did that because it would help me relax, and calm my mind because I know it's all in His hands. Maybe if you find a favorite verse you may like, you could do the same thing, or make a painting of it so you can always remind yourself about it.

"Call to me and I will answer you and tell you great and unsearchable things you do not know." This verse, Jeremiah 33:3, speaks to me: If you call on His name, worship Him, and pray to Him, He will give you an answer. He will help you and guide you and lead you to extraordinary things. He will take you on adventures that you didn't know could happen. He can make the unknown, known. He will take you on journeys, and some with long pathways, some with short. It's all a part of His process, and how He wants it to unfold.

I asked a couple of family members to share their favorite verses with me, and this is what they told me: "For I know the plans I have for you declares the Lord plans to prosper you and not to harm you plans for a hope and future"—Jeremiah 29:11. My cousin told me what this passage says to her: "As teenagers, most of us fear our future, what's going to happen and if it's going to go how we have been dreaming about it our whole lives. Thinking about my future as it is coming up very soon this verse gives me a lot of peace and hope that God knows what's in store for my life and He has already planned it according to His will and not mine. He assures me that His will shall be done."

Revelation 21:4 NIV says: "He will wipe every tear from their eyes. There will be no more death or mourning or crying or pain, for the old order of things has passed away." Therefore, we're always confident and know that as long as we're at home in the body we are away from the Lord. For we live by faith, not by sight. This verse relates to the subject of death and loss. These past couple of years I have experienced back-to-back losses of people who I loved with all my heart. It has been a tough couple of years but all of those people were believers, and that verse gives me a sense of peace and hope in knowing that they are present with the Lord and that they would rather be there. When a believer passes away, Heaven rejoices even though we mourn. God gives us comfort in knowing that they're in His presence.

My mother's favorite verse is, 1."The Lord is my shepherd. I shall not want. 2. He maketh me to lie down in green pastures: He leadeth me beside the still waters. 3. He restoreth my soul: He leadeth me in the paths of righteousness for his name's sake. 4. Yea, though I walk through the valley of the shadow of death, I will fear no evil: for thou art with me; thy rod and thy staff they comfort me. 5. Thou prepares a table before me in the presence of. mine enemy: thou anoints my head with oil; my cup runneth over. 6. Surely goodness and mercy shall follow me all the days of my life: and I will dwell in the house of the Lord for ever."—Psalms 23:1-6. My mother likes the opening of this verse because it reminds her of how good God is, and that He is her Lord. He will take care of all her needs, and most of her wants. Everything he does for her is for her good. It also lets her know that he will be with her even through death and that she should not be afraid, because He's always there. When my Mother reads or speaks this verse she feels comforted in knowing that she is a child of the most highest God.

There are a couple of things that I go by that are not Bible verses, but my religious belief confirms these. For example, I believe everything happens for a reason. I'm a firm believer in this; I believe that if something was meant to be, it will happen. If God wants something to happen, then it will happen. If you were supposed to go to that soccer game to watch your friend play, and it was cancelled, maybe it was cancelled for your own good. Maybe you weren't supposed to be out there because of the thunder and lightning.

On your last day of school you were late due to traffic and you were very upset about being late. But when you arrived you learned that there had been a school shooting and if you had been on time you could have been killed. Then you know being late is what was supposed to happen to you that day to save your life. If you were competing in a gymnastics competition and you broke your foot, your first reaction is anger because now you have to be out for the entire sports season. There was a reason this happened to you but it is not obvious right away; it is revealed later or you may never know. But regardless, you have to remain positive and think about all the time you will have to train for your next competition/tournaments. You don't let this set you back, this is the moment to pick yourself back up and tell yourself that you still have another chance to get to that first place.

You trust in Him and God will lead you into the right way. He will always be right by your side to guide you every step of the way. You can choose to see a moment as a setback, and be all sad, angry, and doubt yourself about it. Or you can pick yourself back up, and make every second of your recovery count. So I believe everything happens for a reason. There are multiple things that can happen to you, and you may not know why they're happening, but believe me, there is a reason. If you have a positive mindset, then you will have positive outlook no matter what happens. You should always trust Him.

Another thing I go by is: "God is greater than my highs and my lows." God is greater than anything. He will always be there when you hit highs in your life, and He will most definitely be there when you hit your lowest points. You can explore, open the Bible and learn who He is. He is such a powerful person and getting to know Him is one of the greatest things you can do. When I was eight years old, I was inspired to get baptized in my church. I was amazed and wanted to give my life to Jesus. As I got older, about thirteen or fourteen, I wanted to know more about Him. So, I made that my priority to explore. I read the Bible more, and then realized that I wanted to dedicate my life to Him again. I realized that I didn't understand and know Him like I wanted to. Don't get me wrong, when I was younger I knew Him. And went to church every Sunday, and knew that He died on the cross for our sins, but I don't think I fully understood it the way I do now.

Growing older, reading about Him more makes me feel full inside, and open up to Him. Having a relationship with Him, and knowing that I can count on him every second of the day is comforting. These verses helped me through that way. I'm still learning so much more about Him everyday. Your words are more powerful than any negativity coming your way. He will be there with you when you're happy, sad, alone, and lost. All you have to do is call upon His name. There can be many ways to call upon His name, whether it's a verse, if you need to pray, or if you need to pull out your Bible and start reading. I have some favorite songs as well for those times when I'm in a mood where I need to just sit down and hear His words. If you're feeling weak, or when you hit rock bottom, you can play some of your favorite worship songs. A great song can always lift you up, even if you need to get something off your shoulders. Music can speak to your heart and make you feel alive, free, and uplifting. Some days you just need to sit down, relax, and take the words you're reading, the song you're listening to, or the pictures you're drawing according to the Word and meditate on them.

This goes the same with reading his Word, reading his word can bring you back alive and on your feet, so when you need that extra energy seek Him. I know people who like reading His words, and drawing pictures off to the side to help them capture and a way to really understand the Word. All people are different and like serving Him differently, and that is what is so fascinating: how people worship differently. God made everyone different in his or her own way. Building a relationship with God is important, especially as a teen/young adult, because once you get out in the real world you will see how much you need Him in your life. You cannot direct your relationship into the spiritual level if you haven't reached it personally yet. Before imposing this goal into a relationship, strengthen your own faith and relationship with yourself. He can only work in your relationship if you let Him work in you first. Making sure that you work truly on yourself and that you're in a good state of mind before growing that relationship. If you and other people in your life want to grow even more in a relationship too, pray for them. Reading the Word and understanding will not be easy for them. If they are getting frustrated with themselves, pray for them, as you will both grow. If that person has gone through some difficulties it may be hard for them. Once you become older you will need to solve problems and know how to handle them.

There are some unkind, rude, and selfish people out in the world. We simply can't control what happens but you can get through this. There will be some challenging days and you might be confused on how to handle it the right way. Call on His name and ask Him how you should handle this sticky situation. Even as a teen, He has taught me many lessons. Getting older and knowing Him can teach you a lot of things. How I need to respect my parents, elderly, and others around me. As I grow up, I'm realizing that I'm so beyond blessed to have a relationship with Him. He has given me so many opportunities that I would never have even imagined. Opening up doors left and right. Get involved with a group of individuals who want to know as much as you want to help. You can make it fun. Meet at a quiet restaurant, library, church, coffee shop, mostly where it is comfortable for you. It's your time out of the day, or week to sit down and open up. Don't let anything get in the way of you and the Lord's time. You can ask God for anything, you can ask Him to change your bad attitude, need for perfection, to stop living in the past and not looking forward, and to not give up when things become difficult. Asking Him to help you and guide you to the right way doesn't hurt, and it doesn't make you any less of a person. We all need help. Nobody's perfect. No one has a perfect life; we all have our struggles. There's no such thing as perfect. Focus on what you can do well instead of making every little detail match your imagination. We have a limited amount of time, so it's best to use that time wisely. It's nice to live in the past and to think about memories, but you cannot literally *live* in the past. Look forward and see what your goals are in life and how to get there. Take that first footstep; ask God for guidance. There can be both too much and too little of looking forward to the future. You might give up on things because it's too hard or you believe that what you want to achieve takes up too much time. How will that attitude help you? Don't you want to succeed? Don't you want your dreams to come true? Don't you want to look back and say, "Yes, I did that"? Don't let your dreams drift away because you think they're too difficult. Nothing in this world comes easy. We all feel like giving up at times; that's Him testing you. So asking for help doesn't hurt; it shows that you want to become better.

Chapter 6

Who are you?

Are you a positive or negative person? Kind or nice? Outgoing or not outgoing? Likeable or not likeable? Do you ever sit back and ask yourself who are you sometimes? Are you one to be productive? I think everyone should have a balance, but I like to be productive as much as possible. Create goals; don't think it's too early to think about your future. As you get older, contemplate your hobbies, interests, and passion for what you want to do. If you know what you want to do, you can see what you need to do to get there. Be a positive person and make goals.

When my brother was in high school he made a goal that he was going to be different from the rest of his friends in school. He made the effort and time, and blocked everything that was slowing him down in achieving his goals. With one year at the West Point Prep School and then the four requirement years; five years later, he graduated from West Point Military Academy, and now is in the U.S. Army. When he look back on those years and he can see how much more he's doing with his life compared to others his age. He looks back and see that some of the people he went to school with are still living at their parent's house, haven't gone to college, and aren't as successful as he is now. It all started with him setting goals, and cutting out things that weren't going to help him get where he wanted to be.

Are you a neat person or a messy person? You may want to take some time out and clean your room. Get rid of the stuff you don't want or need. Bookshelf or closet, try to organize everything neatly so that you have a good and clean surrounding. Staying neat and organized as a teen can help you as you get older. Get rid of things you don't need or want anymore. Sell things online and make some extra money. Don't we all love that? So instead of piling up things in your room, just sell some things online. There are tons of resources out there that can help you do this (Amazon for books and CDs, for example). So clean your surroundings, but knowing where your things are for school, sports, and other activities are important. Another positive feature is to be sure you look presentable when you have a meeting for a school event. Make sure you look good! When you present yourself well, it gives the impression that you have pride in your appearance.

Do you want to stay productive and learn something new? Learn how to cook a meal if you don't already know how too. If you don't know how to cook a meal, learn now, because when you get older you will have to cook a meal for your family—or yourself—one day. Learn new information on any topic such as in science, culture, history, media, or something that you're passionate about. We're extremely lucky to have technologies like the Internet to give us access to any information for free. So take this time to learn something new.

The same goes with knowing how to pay bills, earn and manage money, and politely and respectfully talk to adults. So taking time out to learn new things will be a benefit for you as you grow older. If you like a specific subject in school, go online and learn more about it. Be creative. With all this technology nowadays, take advantage of this time, and use it wisely.

So who are you? One to put the time in and learn something new, or one to sit in your room like everyone else? Do you want to be healthier, and exercise more, or sit on the couch and eat and get fat? I know, it sounds so good to sleep in, and be in your bed all day, and eat, but will that help you out in the long run? It sounds like fun, but going outside and getting some fresh air is more productive. Many teenagers these days have been noted to have health troubles and lots of stress. With school, homework, sports, and other activities, life can be stressful. You may want to calm your senses by doing a little meditation, or by going for a stroll or jog; listening to music to become fresh and stress-free also helps. It is a great way to stay fit and to keep your energy level up. You will feel so much better after a nice day, and you can have fun too by doing many of these things—playing soccer, going on a jog, etc.—with friends. Finally, getting enough sleep is also important, and if you don't get enough, it can create more stress for you.

As for reading, I know it can be hard to find a book that grabs your attention. However, reading is essential for improving your concentration and comprehension levels. Reading, by the way, can also include magazines and newspapers, not just novels or history books. As a kid in elementary school, I didn't like reading. I had trouble with reading and didn't find anything really interesting. In middle school it got a tad better. I ended up finding some books I liked, but never really loved reading. Now I have found what's right for me. You may never know what you may wind up being interested in. Anyway, reading is an important skill you will need as you get older, with reading signs, emails, documents, etc. You will always need to read, so I see it as a very important skill to have throughout life.

By the time you become an adult you know a little about yourself and realize what your strengths and weaknesses are. For instance, if you wanted to become a teacher but have difficulty communicating your thoughts to others, this is a perfect time to change that direction or modify your own abilities to meet your goals. If you overcome your fears, you are good to go; if you don't, then maybe it's not your cup of tea. You can change what you desire at any time; just find something that you're comfortable with. Being in your teen years is an excellent time for this. It's all about experimenting. You can experiment with many things, with what you like, what type of music you like, who you want to hang out with, what sports you like, and what you even want to be when you grow up.

Learn how to drive if you haven't already. Explore more of your town or state; step outside of your comfort zone. Whether that means speaking publicly, sharing your painting, a song, a book, share what you love to do. Experience with life as a teen. It is absolutely acceptable for teens to change their style whenever they feel like it. We call those periods of change "phases" and we all go through many of them, no matter how embarrassing it is to look back at them. So do you want to experience and explore? What is great about being a teenager is that you have more room to make mistakes. Chances are good that you won't be penalized for not knowing better. Therefore, get some experience, which can be viewed as practice before you're in the real world on your own. Be a teen, make mistakes—but learn from those mistakes. Now, I'm not saying make *huge* mistakes, but use common sense as well. It's okay if you get in a little trouble, because you might need to get in a little trouble to learn. Make mistakes, and see what the effects are before going out into the real world.

Are you going to be a person to pick someone else up when they are down? Some teens go through more depression than others. We all have different lives and different lifestyles. Some teens who are bullied go through changes in sleep patterns, eating habits, experience a declined interest in normal and healthy activities, and grades drop in school and college.

If they prefer isolation and being alone, those are signs of depression. Being observant toward these signs at an early stage may help to block/stop further damage and guide them toward healthy ways of dealing with their concerns. So reach out to them, and show them you are there for them. Take it one step at time. If they ask you not to talk to anyone else about their situation, respect them. Showing a person you have respect and can be trusted is important. Slowly offer the help they need. If they don't ask for it, you should be the bigger person and get them the proper help they need, and talk to them about it. You shouldn't judge or criticize their feelings or thoughts. Being sensitive toward them and the fact that they are exposed to a range of emotions is an important step in understanding their transition. Anger, confusion, jealousy, and dislike toward things they dislike can be signs they are going through numerous emotions themselves. Making sure that the person is safe to talk to you. It's important that he or she knows that they are worthy. Will you be that person to help someone else? Will you make them feel safe? Are you the one who plays sports, the one who stays up all night to study for a test the next day, or the one who loves to learn new things? The one who is outgoing and who encourages others to be the best that they can be and to love the teen years? Enjoy these moments while you're still a teen. Have fun, especially while you're in high school, and in college. Those times will only come around once. Life is an adventure—and such a rollercoaster!

Chapter 7

The shadows of my older brother

I have an older brother, his name is Haven, and we are extremely close. We're about ten years apart. There can be many pros and cons about having an older sibling. I have no other siblings; it is just the two of us. I remember like it was yesterday how we would go to Sweet Frog, the movies, the bowling alley, the mall, and the pool together. We would do everything together. He was my best friend in the entire world. I could talk to him about anything. We would play video games together and pretend we were playing the guitar together. When it was time for the holidays we would make cookies, cakes, and treats for the family. One holiday I made mint chocolate chip cookies, and he and I ate the entire batch. He always made jokes, and he always knew how to put a smile on my face, whether it was from making funny noises or going on a run for ice cream. Then sadly it became time for him to graduate high school. I hated to see him go off to college. I was only in the third grade going into fourth grade when he graduated from high school. We had a short summer together because he received an appointment from the Senate to attend the Military Academy at West Point, New York. He left early before the Fourth of July. We all went with him to get him settled in his new room. The day we dropped him off was really bad for me. You see, West Point gave us five minutes to say goodbye. I was not expecting that, and all I was thinking about was what I could say in five minutes. I was holding back the tears and I knew my Mom was holding back her tears. Well, we said our farewells. The next time we saw him he was in uniform and his head was bald. They had shaved all his hair off. We could only see him. We could not talk to him. I tried to sneak a wave to him but I don't think he saw me. So we left to go back home. It was a six-hour ride, so I slept most of the way back home.

I finished the summer on the swim team without my brother that year. Other people would ask me about him because he was a lifeguard at that pool, and he taught private swim lessons. Once the school year started I was a little better because I had to focus on my work. Also, the gymnastics season started and that helped me not to think about him so much also. My brother didn't get a chance to come home too often and when he did it was a six-hour bus ride for him. I missed him tons, and it was hard for us to talk to each other because he was always busy with studying or doing military things. I started to find pros and cons of being in his shadows. One pro was helping me with my homework, which helped me to get all A's. He used to drive me places and we would get good food to eat. We baked treats together for us to eat. He was always there for me when I got in trouble with my parents. He could talk to my parents for me and they would listen to him so I rarely got in trouble. He helped me out with my future plans, like what classes I should take in high school. He always encouraged me to do my best and be my best. My brother helped me when I needed someone to give me an extra push. He always looked out for me.

I remember when I was in middle school, and didn't feel like doing my work, we made a bet and I paid him money to do my work. I really hope my teacher isn't reading this—LOL. Then he explained what he did and showed me the steps so I would know how to do it if I had to do it without him. I got an A, so hey, I guess it worked! So if you have an older sibling, they can come in handy with quite a few things.

I loved hanging out with my big brother and cooking together. It was our favorite thing to do together. I remember one time he and I were fighting with the pillows in the living room, and it didn't go well. My Mom had two white lamps that she hand-carried on the plane from Korea. She loved those lamps and had them for a long time. Our parents were gone somewhere that day and my brother and I started playing together, hitting each other with the pillows. Since our parents weren't there, things got a little wild and out of hand. The next thing we new we hit one of the lamps and it fell on the floor and broke. Haven said to me, Mom is going to kill us. We have to try and fix this lamp. Then the light bulb came on, and we decided if we put tape on it she wouldn't notice. So we went to her office and we pulled out the tape. I was holding the broken pieces, while he taped it up. We sat the lamp back on the table with the taped side to the wall. The lamped look like nothing was wrong with it.

When Mom came home we decided not to mention anything about the broken lamp. My brother and I kept that as out little secret. Months later, Mom was cleaning up and noticed when she tried to pick it up she felt the tape. She looked at the lamp and thought it looked a little different from the other matching one. Then she looked a little closer and saw a crack. She turned it all the way around, and saw the tape around it, and called us downstairs. She asked us if we knew what happened, and we were smirking, and told her we didn't know. That's when she knew it was us. You know, the funniest thing was Mom was not angry with us at all. She ended up laughing with us. So then we realized we did a lot of preparing for the day when Mom would find out for nothing because she didn't get angry with us at all.

You know, even if we were to get in trouble, my brother would obviously take the blame, because that's the brother I know. When I was in middle school and people would bully me, I would always talk to him about it, and he would help me a lot with that. He told me something that I will always take with me: "Who are they, they are no bodies." They are just some middle school kids, who need to grow up, and they don't know what they're talking about. They think they know so much but they don't and they aren't worth your time.

Bullies are just people who need people to love them; they just want to drag other people down, because people dragged them down once or more times before. In the long run, they're a bunch of nobodies who want to bully others. So if you're dealing with bullies, just think to yourself "Who are they?"

When I was going into high school, he would set out the classes I should take. He always looked out for me with physical aspects, and educational aspects. When I needed that extra push, he was the one who told me that I needed to get something done. Whether it was to go on a run, or to sit down and get my homework done. He cares so much for me. One day I was excited to see him because we were going to go somewhere. I was running up the stairs, and put my backpack in my room. I was running into his room with socks on. Boom, I tripped over his rug and fell and hit my chin on his bed. I was crying super hard, I think I was so loud that people on Mars could hear me. He hurried and picked me up and sat me upon his bed so he could take a look at it. He told me it looked real bad so he picked me up, and rushed downstairs to tell our parents. So they decided to take me to the hospital, and there we were on the way to the hospital. I kind of thought it was cool after a little. I knew I was going to get ice cream at the end so I knew I would be a cool kid. So we ran into the emergency room, and I got all fixed up, and ready to go home. On the way home, we all stopped by to get ice cream, so it was a win for my brother and me. We went home, and went on about our day. Looking back on it, my brother was there for me from the time I was running into his room, to leaving the hospital, and getting ice cream. Still to this day I still have a scar on the bottom of my chin. I remember it fondly because it was about those fun times we had.

To sum up, he was always there for me, and to this day we still have such a fun bond. Not *always* fun, as there were some cons to growing up in the shadows of Haven Langston Barner. He was extremely smart, a very good competitive swimmer, and respectful. Needless to say I had some big shoes to fill coming up behind him. So when he left, it was great pressure on me if I would be going to an Academy or not. Everyone asked me, and I didn't know what to say and still don't know.

Because you see, I'm only in the ninth grade right now, and graduating from high school seems like a long ways from now. I just felt like coming behind him with his high standards was so much for me to live up too. I feel like people who have older siblings can relate. I was never the kid to take super high classes. I just wanted to take whatever I needed to take to get in to a good college. I thought I had to do exactly what my brother did. He was a competitive swimmer, but I didn't like swimming as much, so I did gymnastics.

However, I decided to step away from it in the eighth grade. Then I tried track and decided to take a break from that as well. I started to compare myself to my brother. I thought I was never going to make people happy. I felt discouraged, and it made me sad. I wanted people to be happy with any decision I made. I thought when I grew up, went off to college, and announced where I was going to go, I wouldn't have people looking down on me. I didn't want people telling me to my face "oh you're going there, that's cool" but then talking bad about me behind my back, and saying "she didn't go to the Academy like her brother." Maybe she doesn't have the high standards as he did. I always thought about this, and it would make me feel extremely angry. When I was in middle school I would tell myself, "Okay, high school is coming up, so you need to be as good as Haven, if not even better." So I would drill this in my head, and always thought this was a competition whether I was going to be "the better one."

I knew from the start that my brother was going to a prestigious school. I wanted my own name, for people to think of me as Gabriella Barner, and that I would also go to a prestigious university. I didn't want to become just his little sister. I struggled with that ever since he was in his last year of college, and I just now started to realize that I wouldn't ever be my brother and that I won't be like him. If people think differently of me, they can go ahead and think that. We are two completely different people. I told myself

42

that I am my own person. I can act nor try to be like someone else. It simply won't work, and as soon as I started realizing that, I felt better about myself. I started to believe in myself, and tell myself I would still be successful and that I would still do something in life. If this is you, I am telling you: be *yourself*, not anyone else. You will still do something great with your life. Go for your dreams and don't live in the shadows of someone else. This doesn't go just for making your own name; this goes for numerous other topics. Be yourself, don't change yourself for someone you're not. Act and be yourself. People are going to look at you for yourself, and love the real you. Especially for teen girls, I know you see those "perfect Instagram influencers." Trust me, they are not perfect. You see a little bit of their life and so you get maybe only three quarters of what they're all about. The other fourth you don't see. They might be going through tough times, are sick, whether mentally or physically, or even both. They're other things they could be going through as well. So yes, they do have highlights, and that's what we see, but just know that they are human as well.

Everyone has highs and lows, so there's no such thing as being perfect. At the end of the day, be yourself, and don't try to change yourself for anyone. I was extremely happy for my brother, but it came with struggles. At times I thought I could be him, but I found out that I have to find myself and it may not look like what he's doing. But whatever it is, it will be what I want to do, not what others want me to do. Don't worry about what your life looks like to other people. You have to do what is best for you. Keep everything in perspective and remember: There is only one of you, so show the world what *you* can offer. Go get it!!

Chapter 8

Adoption

Adoption. Let's talk about it. It's interesting, cool, nice, and amazing. It can be different things to different people. I see adoption as an interesting way of caring for others. In fact, I am adopted. I was adopted when I was around one year old. I can't speak for everyone's adoption story but this is mine. The story I was told is funny, but I will get to that later.

My Mom was the first one in the family who thought about adopting. She wanted a daughter. She talked to my Dad and he thought it would be a good idea to look into it. So my Mom then asked my brother what he thought about it. He was only nine years old at the time and he was happy about the idea of having a sibling. She wanted to know how he felt about having a little sister. He liked the idea. He found it pretty cool, and he was on board. So they started the research process.

My Mom found an agency (Bethany Christian Services) that had been in the adoption business for more than 50 years. She contacted the agency and signed up for the first meeting. My brother and my Mom went to the first meeting together to get all the information. My Mom told my Dad about what needed to be done to adopt a child. My Dad was all in as well and excited about the thought of having a daughter. After my Mom and Dad talked about it, they decided they had only three criteria for adoption and that was: the baby had to be a girl, under three years old, and healthy. They didn't care where the child came from (meaning what state) or the child's nationality.

My parents just wanted a healthy little girl. As they started the process they soon found out there weren't many healthy babies in the United States or that the young mothers in the program were looking for much younger parents than my Mom and Dad. So they decided to look at another country for a daughter. Bethany Christian had a very strong and promising adoption program with the country of Guatemala. My parents decided to apply for the Guatemala program. Yes, that is where I am from: Guatemala City, Guatemala.

Within two months the adoption agency contacted my parents with pictures of beautiful little baby girls. They were all anywhere from two to four weeks old. There was one picture of a little girl who stood out from the rest. She was wrapped up tight in a blanket with her eyes closed. She had beautiful brown skin; dark jet-black straight hair; and she had one hand sticking up from the blanket as if to say, "Choose me." When my Mom, Dad, and brother saw that picture they fell in love with me right away. They all agreed I would fit in perfectly, and for Mom, Dad, and Haven to be my forever family.

The rest is history. Fast forward, they got to the end of the adoption process (it took over a year and a lot of money), and it was time to get on a plane to go pick me up and bring me home. When my forever family arrived, they stayed in the Marriott in Guatemala City. It was very modern and even had a McDonald's next door. The foster family that I was staying with brought me to the hotel to meet my new family. My Mom and Dad told me that when they first saw me they thought I was so beautiful. I came to them right away with no hesitation. I stayed with them in the hotel for two weeks before going back to the United States.

It took that long to get all the legal papers and my passport. During the long wait, my parents toured Guatemala. They told me how gorgeous the countryside really is. It is called the "Land of Eternal Spring." They saw beautiful plants full of bright colors and the weather was like spring everyday. It was in December and they visited many churches that had beautiful nativity scenes. The statues in the nativity scenes were dressed in elaborate clothing. It was so beautiful they took lots of pictures. The nights were warm, the air was a breeze on their arms, and it was all you would ever imagine. They had tons of fun. I often find myself looking back on the pictures, wishing I could remember those days. Even with all the beauty of Guatemala, there were many poor people. They saw how the majority of the people lived and it was not good. Some people lived in boxes, on the mountainside without running water. People were homeless and needed food. After seeing how much the people of Guatemala needed help, my parents were so grateful that they were able to give me a whole new better life.

The day for me to travel to the United States finally came June 14, 2006. My Mom and I had first class seats, and I was given all kinds of toys, milk, and baby snacks. I was so happy. I ate and played until I went to sleep. My Mom told me that I slept most of the way. I was a good baby to travel with no problems at all.

Once we arrived in the United States the airline stewardess said to me "welcome home." As soon as we got off the plane my Dad had someone to take a picture of all of us to document my first day in the United States. We got to the car and then drove home. My brother played with me on the way home. I think we were so glad to have each other.

The rest is truly history. I just want to say that adoption was the best thing that could have ever happened to me. I do think about my birth mother from time to time just like I'm sure she thinks about me because that is normal. But I truly believe my birth mother loved me so much and wanted me to have a better life. She had no other option but adoption. God directs our path and He gave me a forever family and I will always cherish and love them.

46

The ladies on my Mom's job wanted to give my Mom a baby shower. They all came over to our house with lots of gifts, mostly toys and clothes for me. We had food, drinks, and a big cake. It was fun for my Mom, but she said I was a little scared of all the people, so she held me most of the time. Growing up my brother loved to take care of me. He wanted to hold me all the time. He soon started to feed me, clothed me, and read to me. We would have sleepovers all the time, and my Mom saw how much he loved to have a little sister. That was the beginning of how we got super close, and we're still close to this day. I tell people all the time that as soon as my brother and I saw each other for the first time we both had a connection. We played games together and had lots of fun. I remember one of my best times was when we pretended playing the guitar together.

Let's fast-forward a few years, to about when I was seven or eight years old. I noticed that I looked a little different from my Mom. I had straight hair and my Mom's hair was curly. I had brown skin and my Mom was fair skinned. I asked my Mom why I didn't look like her one day, and she then explained to me. At first, I didn't really understand. I just knew that they were people who took me in when I needed it. As I got older, I asked more questions. Then one day I finally understood what adoption was all about and why they did what they did. My Mom soon told me the full story of the process, and I still ask questions to this day.

My first initial thought when I found out was a mix emotion of confusion, happiness, and sadness. There were a hundred questions that went through my mind. Who are my parents? Why did they give me up? What are their names? Do I have any other sisters and brothers now? I was happy, I was a little sad because I didn't know, and still to this day don't know who they are.

There isn't one day that passes by that I don't think about my birth parents. I know there are other people who are adopted. I also know people get adopted for many different reasons. Kids could be removed from parents who have mental health, drug, and alcohol problems. It could be a situation where they didn't have people to take care of them, they were in a bad environment, and there are many other reasons as well. At first I was nervous, scared, and embarrassed to share with others that I'm adopted. I didn't want people to think of me as weird. I wanted to be normal and have a regular life. I didn't ever bring up the fact that I was. It felt like a bandage: You think it will hurt when you rip it off, but it's really only for a second or two. I initially thought my adoption was something that I should be ashamed of. I didn't want to tell anyone when I was younger, and wanted this fact to be kept in the family. For a long time I told my Mom that I didn't feel comfortable telling people I was adopted.

My Mom said she would not tell anyone and that she would leave that up to me. My friends didn't know, I told one of my best friends when I was around thirteen, and she thought it was so interesting. I then became more open about it. I became more grateful, and happy. I told my Mom that I told someone, and she told me that I can share whatever I want with people, that I never had to ask for permission. I started to tell some of my other friends, but there are still people to this day that I know who don't know. It's not that I don't want them to know. It's that I didn't think it was necessary to talk about it. If they asked, I told them who I was, but mostly I would never go and tell them. I knew I kept it very private from my peers for a while.

When I started to tell people, I got mostly positive reactions. While I was in school people started to say nasty, rude things out loud, and it was directly toward me. Then they would make it known, and say them directly to me. They would say how my birth parents didn't love me, no one cared for me, and that I was a nobody. I kept that inside of me for a long time, and didn't tell anyone.

There are just so many nasty people out here. I kept this on my shoulders and kept on thinking how people truly didn't love me. I use to think my birth Mom didn't love me because she gave me up, and she didn't care for me. I thought she thought I was going to be a nobody. I thought she didn't want

48

me anymore. I constantly had thoughts like that running through my mind. I started to let those people get to me. I was scared to talk about my family when all the other kids talked about their parents. People would come up to me, and say to me, "You look nothing like your parents."

For adoptees, there's a lot of shame that comes with being adopted: guilt, sadness, and low self-esteem about your identity. It isn't easy knowing you came from another family and not understanding why, not being able to have answers, and feeling unloved when you have to talk about it. I hope that people would be more sensitive to adoptees and be careful how they address questions. Some questions can cause nothing but pain and emotional distress and is highly insensitive.

I have tons of questions myself. The biggest: Why did my birth mother give me up? I know deep down in my heart she did the best thing she could for me. I thank her because I would not be here on this Earth if it weren't for her. It took a lot for her to not be able to see me grow up. She cared for me, she loved me, but mostly she wanted to give me a better life. If I were still living in Guatemala, I might not have had the many opportunities that I have today living in the United States. Growing up and thinking about my birth mother, I feel even more loved, and grateful, because she wanted the best for me.

Again, I can't speak for everyone, but if you're in my situation, just know that your mother loved you so much she gave you up. It might be hard to deal with at first but it took me a while to understand why she did what she did. It took me a good eight to nine years to finally figure out why. Why this, why that, it all came to me one day. Each and every adoption story and situation is unique; it's our story, express it. There is so much involved. Some adoptees are truly happy with their adoptive families. Others are not. I didn't ask to be adopted but now looking back on it, I'm glad my birth mother made that decision. We didn't openly invite feelings of rejection and abandonment into our lives, nor would we ever.

Some of us grew up wondering if we were wanted. What we did wrong? What was wrong with us? Nothing. Did they love me? Yes. Just know that they gave you up to create a better place for yourself so that you can go out in this crazy world, and explore, and live life as a new adventure, so you could better yourself, and so you don't have to end up in their shoes. To want to give a kid the life I had or better is such a beautiful and generous thing. I grew up with my parents; some may not. Some of you all out there could have been adopted when you were older or as a teenager. When you're older it can be hard because when you're no longer a young child it means you have been informed and influenced by many more things.

"Sometimes I wish I was adopted." I've heard people say those seven words, and it's absolutely horrible. To say this is not funny. Being adopted isn't a joke or something anyone should actively wish for. Adoption is not an easy fix, or something that should be used to explain XYZ. Unfortunately, I grew up hearing some family friends say this about their children to dismiss strange behavior. Siblings said it about each other too. They never knew how much it stung me.

Many adoptees are sensitive about their background and origins. It is never ok to make humorous jabs about adoption. Being adopted doesn't mean there's a problem or that something is wrong with the adoptee. Be sensitive and considerate of others' feelings. Joking around about adoption is not acceptable behavior in front of an adoptee.

To be honest, I would say I'm extremely grateful that I have parents who love me and took me in as their own, but I do wish it worked out with my birth parents. I wish that my parents had worked things out and were able to take care of me. If I could go back and help them out, I would. Adoption happens without our consent. We never asked for it, but it was given to us to be loved.

"Blood isn't everything." My adopted family is my family. Don't refer to my biological family as my "real" family. It is complicated forever. Trying to figure out who I am and where I fit in is a daily thing for the rest of my life. Every person deals with it differently. Blood isn't everything. I know that is hard to believe and understand for people who have only known family by blood, but I live by it and treat my best friends as family too. Blood isn't everything, and just because I'm not blood related doesn't mean I don't feel close to my forever family. They are my parents, and my brother, and extended family. My entire family is full of love, and support. There are some things to not mention to people who are adopted. Words can change a person's life, for better or for worse. When the impact is negative, sometimes the damage is so deep that it can't be undone. Words once spoken can't be taken back. Try to uplift a person who especially trusts you so that they can share precious moments with you.

I asked my cousin what adoption meant to her, about what she thinks about when she hears adoption, and this is what she said: "Adoption is the action of raising a non-biological child who wasn't able to be taken care of by their biological parents. So God sends other people to help raise them because it takes a village to raise a child. I see adoption as a great human action that can completely change someone's life for the better. Although a lot of kids come from sad and hard situations it impacts the kids life and future forever."

When I heard her say this I thought how interesting and heart-warming. This sums it up: God will always send someone to the rescue. For me it was my forever family. For my Mom and Dad it was a forever daughter. For my brother it was a forever sister. I know some didn't have a chance to say their goodbyes; some didn't get to say their hellos, but just know that everything happens for a reason. One day, dream to meet your parents, siblings, grandma, or fix any situations you may have. It might not come easy, because trying to solve a problem like this is difficult.

Chapter 9

Covid-19

Where to start? This is such a crazy world we live in today. I was in high school when the coronavirus outbreak occurred. I remember just like it was yesterday, I was in school, about to go on spring break. I went to school like any other regular days, taking it for granted, like most of us. I got up around 6:00 A.M. to get ready. I grabbed a breakfast bar and ran out the door.

It takes me so long in the morning, so I always give myself a decent amount of time to get ready. I still saw myself sprinting out the door to hop in the car. I was on my way to school, and for some reason my Mom and I were being stopped by all the traffic lights. I thought I would never get to school. I walked into school. It was normal, as it was the last minute before my class started.

Sometimes I would just sneak right into the gym and hope no one would notice me walking in. I'm sure at least one person saw me, but I tried my best to be unseen. I went on about my day, going from class to class. As soon as I arrived at my second block class, an email was sent out. My Mom texted me that they were getting emails that students needed to clean out their lockers because after spring break they weren't sure if the students would be going back to school. All of this because of the fast spread of the coronavirus. The school was going to throw away any items left in lockers and the school doors would be locked until further notice. My Mom really got my attention and I was concerned. I was one of the lucky ones because I thought I didn't have anything in my locker. My friend went to her gym locker, and then I figured I'd go to check too. So then I started to realize that I had shoes, a jacket, and a textbook in my locker. It was good that I went with her because if I hadn't, my things would have been thrown away. I almost forgot I had to take my final for math. I was on top of the world after hearing we may not be going back to school after spring break. All I had left to do was just to take my two finals, and then be out.

Later in the day, I went to my third block, and went to class, and left. Then I had lunch. I had such a good time joking around at the lunch table with my friends. I didn't eat lunch, which is normal for me most days. I never realized why, but then I figured it out it's because I snacked during the day.

So by the time I had lunch, I wasn't hungry. Then I went to my last class of the day and took my exam. I was extremely nervous for that exam; I just tried not to fail. I knew if I didn't get at least a B, I really needed to pay attention for the rest of the year. Next, I was about one of the first people done, so that didn't give me a good sign, but hey, yolo. Then, I put my ear buds in and I slumped.

My friend decided to wake me up, I'm glad she did or I actually would have slept through the bell. Then, it was time to go home, walk out, taking everything for granted. Told my teacher I'll see her after spring break, not knowing I wouldn't see her after that day. I met up with my friends after school like we usually do, and hung out until I left to go home. I was there with a good friend, talking, and then I noticed that teacher after teacher was going to a meeting. We stood there and talked about how we were going to hang out soon. Then, there I was on my way home and being so happy that we were on spring break. I can sleep in, and I don't have to worry about being stressed, no tests, or homework for a week. I was so happy to get just a week off, to relax, and take some time off. Where I live, the governor of my state announced all schools K-12 were going to be closed for two weeks. We still didn't stress, we would just get an extra week off, nothing too serious.

Little did I know that this was going to go by so fast. So we were all enjoying our break, and then March 23 came around and the governor announced that we were on lockdown until June 10. That's when we all noticed that this was getting serious pretty quickly. We then realized that we would never see some of our friends anymore because some people were moving, some teachers we loved were leaving, spring sports were over, some first, and some lasts. We would never get to finish out our year; we wouldn't have classes with our best friends. I took it for granted for sure. I had no idea that saying "I'll see you tomorrow" wouldn't be true.

Someone I went to school with since elementary school was getting ready to play softball, and her older sister, a senior, was on the team as well. I could just imagine their excitement to be on the same team together. In a blink of an eye, it was gone.

For the seniors, their proms were gone, graduation, senior pranks, everything. Many took different routes: going into the military, going to a four-year college, or starting a business. For some that was their last time they would be with their classmates. This was their year, and it was taken from them because of a virus. My friend was excited and looking forward to her last prom. This was the class of 2020. It was their year to show off all their hard work; for 12 years they had been waiting for this moment. They couldn't wait to do their senior walk across the stage with their heads up high and to tell themselves that they did it. It was taken from them. For some people who did sports, it was their senior season and they were going to show how far they had come since being a freshman. They were ready to win that title and bring home first place for their team. It never happened.

I speak for others and myself when I say that we all took it for granted. So never take anything for granted. Make sure you tell your loved ones you love them. Make sure you tell that person their shirt looks nice on them. You never know if you will see them again.

For some students, school was their safe place because for some of them it was hard being at home and knowing they had to stay home for the rest of the year. Some have abusive parents, their parents can't provide food, and they are scared to cry out for help. This is reality. You may not think it is, but it's true. This is life: Some students did call school their home. You should try to contact those students, and help them, if you know they need help, contact them, and tell them that they will be okay.

For those seniors in college, their graduation is what they had been looking forward to. Not only did they go to college as a student, but also they represented their college as a student athlete. They have put in tons of hours in studying and training, and they have worked tremendously hard. For some their season was cut short. Some were recruited, and some were walk-ons but they may not get a chance to play right away.

This was their last year, and they wouldn't be able to do what they loved after this year. It's their last time to be with their class before they faced the real world and what's out there for them. It's been rough for sure for many of them, so tell them they will get through it, that they can't always control what life has brought to them.

Once everything gets better, every mall will be open, every restaurant, movie, and concert will be sold out. We have to face the struggles before we can get to the fun, and it takes everyone's input. Pray for all of the first responders and the backstage we don't see. For example, nurses have to face someone new everyday with the virus, risking their lives. Help them out as much as possible; they will be the ones at the end of the day who make sure you're okay.

Although Covid-19 has its lows, it can reach many highs as well. Yes, I've messed up my sleep schedule; I think most of us have during this time. But I've also really taken this time for myself. I've been feeling more confident, and showing myself love, and loving myself. I've been working out, going on runs, started some little projects of mine. I've been watching Netflix and doing many other activities during this pandemic. I started running a lot more, and working out as I mentioned, and started challenging myself. I started with little challenges, taking notes, and writing down what I wanted to accomplish. I've also been cooking a lot more. I'm not as stressed and I'm definitely much happier.

I then decided I want to get back on track after a good four weeks off. I made it a priority that I was still going to learn. Learning is very important, especially since we were still in school. I have been attending my online classes, because I need to get some kind of education in. As much as we don't want to, it's boring, but not having some form of learning isn't the best for us. So I attended my class, and took my test, and still acted like I was still in school.

That's simply what I did, and I let nothing get in the way. It's easy to get distracted, and people to distract you, but you have to be committed and determined that you will get it done. So I decided I wanted to do something different. I decided to write about small things, and that took me into writing a book. I let it go, I let the words just flow out, and I'll put the pieces together. So I just did that for each main topic, and I saw how much you could do when you give yourself a little push. It was a process, not easy, never easy. I didn't want it to be easy. If it's easy, how is that going to make me a better person? It's not. If you take an easy route, you're not challenging yourself.

If you pick the hard route now, then later in life the easy route will come your way. I wanted a challenge, so that's what I did, and I was going to get it done. I can say that during this pandemic I have definitely challenged myself in a way I thought I could never do. If you asked me before this pandemic

56

if I could write a book, I would tell you I couldn't. I didn't believe in myself, and I saw it as too hard. You can do the same thing, just challenge yourself, be committed, and get it done.

Another thing I've struggled with is self-love. I've always compared myself to others, and was aware I had friends who looked so beautiful. I would always be so discouraged, and I'd put myself down about it. As I got older, these feelings started to fade away, and then this time I told myself I wanted a change. I knew that I wanted to come out of this more confident, and I wanted to love my body. You have to love yourself before anyone else can love it. I'd thought I could wish that I could just love myself in a blink of an eye. Then I wrote on some paper all the things I didn't like and what I wanted to change. I then balled up the piece of paper and threw it away. I was showing how I threw away my fears. I threw away the hate, what bullies had to say; I erased it from me.

Everyday I'd try to pick one aspect I love about myself. It started from the little things because the little things are the pathways to the bigger picture. I genuinely wanted a change, and that's what I went after. If you're out there and want a change, you can do it too. If you're going through struggles, write them down—and then throw them away. Or if you have something you found and it works for you, then go for it. You have to start somewhere and to set a good foundation for yourself. Covid-19 has also taught me to reconnect to people, such as reaching out to people who you haven't talked to in a while, including family members. Zoom the family because family is important, and making sure everyone was staying safe. I've gotten closer with family and friends. During this pandemic my brother was overseas in Germany, and we talked mostly when he was available. You can take this time to connect, and even reconnect with people you haven't talked to in a while.

During the pandemic, I haven't lost a loved one, and I am blessed for that. If you have, know that you're not the only one; you're with thousands of people. I can't even imagine losing a loved one from a virus. Grieving is hard, but make sure you pick out what you loved about that person. How much that person impacted you, the key elements. It isn't your fault that this happened; no one wanted this to happen. The anger will boil up: Why, why did this happen to him/her? You can take your anger out in many ways, but make sure you find a healthy way. There's a different way to be unhealthy, but grieving can be healthy because they are honest and real emotions coming out.

This can go for anyone, not just for covid-19, but if you lost a loved one from an illness, or an accident, or whatever the situation was, you can use this as well. We all know the "if only" statement: If only I told him/her to stay inside, or if this is another situation, you can't blame yourself for others actions. Guilt often accompanies bargaining. We start to believe there was something we could have done differently to have helped save our loved one. Then there's depression. Again this could go for anyone who has lost a loved one from Covid-19 or another reason. A reaction relating to the loss is that we worry that, in our grief, we have spent less time with others who depend on us. This phase may be eased by simple clarification and reassurance.

Depression is more subtle and, in a sense, perhaps more private. It is our quiet preparation to separate and to bid our loved one farewell. Sometimes all we really need is a hug. So making sure everyone is okay is very important especially if loved ones are lost. The last step is acceptance, and accepting that yes, sadly, he or she is gone because of a virus. I see it as everything happening for a reason. If it was in the books for it to happen, then it was meant to be. Even though that might be harsh to hear, it's true for me. I see it as if that's how God wanted their going to be, then He wanted that to happen.

Others can be there for you and help comfort you through this process. The best thing you can do is to allow yourself to feel the grief as it comes over you. Again, this could go for anything, but during this time hundreds of people were dying because of Covid-19. It's been a tough and rough time for so many people.

Chapter 10

Precious time with loved ones

My family is unique in a certain way. We love to have fun and enjoy the moment. We have our differences, but we all respect each other's opinions. We are a caring, loving family, and if there's one thing we all love to do it is to travel. We love to see different places around the world, learn something new about other countries, what they eat, and their way of life. I absolutely love traveling, and experiencing a unique way of living. We took a huge trip not too long ago to Europe and it was beyond fun. We all made tremendous memories together. We laughed a lot, and it was such an adventure. My mother thinks she loves adventures, but in reality she... well, we all told her that she does. We ended up packing our bags and didn't necessarily have a booked flight. You see, my Dad and Mom are retired military officers and they like to use their benefits (also, my brother had just graduated from the U.S. Military Academy, and he was officially a second lieutenant).

My parents thought it was time to show him the ropes when it came to catching a military airlift using space-A, which means space availability and you can get a free plane trip hopefully to your destination but maybe not—LOL. Let me tell you the story. We each packed a small bag because we knew we wouldn't have much space and never knew how long or how far we would have to walk. We drove to Andrew Air Force Base to hopefully catch a plane to Germany. We parked in the long-term parking area at Andrews's flight area. Parking was free and we could leave the car there for as long as we needed it to be there. We were there for about five hours when we found out that the flight we wanted to get on was full. That was very disappointing but we knew that could happen; it was all a part of the adventure.

There was a nice USO lounge so we went in and claimed a chair. The chairs were nice leather recliners and we had a blanket and decided to get a nap. Later that night one of the sergeants came into the lounge looking for us because he had some good news. He told us that they had a plane going to McGuire AFB, NJ and we could get on that plane because they had plenty of seats. He also told us McGuire had quite a few flights going to Germany on a daily basis. So we agreed and boarded the plane. It was a cargo plane with no cargo except for us. We had to sit on the bucket seats and put earplugs in our ears. Oh, and before I forget to tell you, we had to pay $9.00 per person for our boarding tickets. So $36.00 for a family of four—not too bad, huh? Once we arrive at McGuire AFB we immediately took our passports and signed up to get on the next flight going to Frankfurt, Germany.

We had about a two- to three-hour wait, so we went into the USO to check out what they had. They served food, drinks, games, and a big screen TV to watch while sitting in comfortable chairs. We heard the boarding call for the flight to Germany and grabbed our belongings. We were in the waiting area hoping they would call the Barner family. But again, that flight was not a flight for personnel; it had just come in for a stop to fuel and then had to make other stops to pick up cargo and would not have any room for people. Again we were disappointed but still lifted each other up and reminder each other that we were on an adventure and we'd be happy no matter what happened or were we ended up. So again we made ourselves comfortable in the USO until the next flight was to arrive going to Germany. It was going to be several hours, so we decided to get some rest.

After sleeping for about five hours, one of the sergeants came in to wake us up and said he could get us closer to Germany but not *in* Germany. He had an unexpected flight coming in and that flight had passenger seats and we could get on it. So we asked where is it going? He said "Portugal, the island of Lajes." My Mom looked at my Dad and said "Yes, let's go. I've never been to Portugal." We all looked at each other and my Dad said, "Let me find out more about this Air Base first." So my Dad walked with the sergeant and they talked all about it. It was a well-kept secret that the Air Force had this base. It only had 2,000 airmen assigned there. My Dad came back and told us he signed us up to go and the plane would be landing in one hour to pick us up. We were so excited to finally be going on this trip! We were also excited about seeing a country none of us had ever seen before.

The flight from McGuire AFB to Portugal seemed short because I think we all went to sleep. When we arrived it seemed like a different world because it was dark and it was an air base so a lot of people weren't around. We went through customs and we were free to go. We didn't have a hotel to stay in, so my Dad and brother started asking about where we could stay and a lady told them about the officer's quarters. She contacted a cab and they took us to the officer's quarters. To our surprise the place had been newly renovated and all they had were executive suites. So my Dad got two rooms that were joined together so we all could sleep comfortably in a nice bed. The rooms were so nice, everything brand new and extremely clean. We slept well that night. We all got up early the next morning so we could see what Portugal looked like, especially because of the fact that we were on an island. A military base on an island—how cool! We walked over to the officer's club for breakfast. It was absolutely beautiful. The water was a crystal blue, the grass was a beautiful green, and the sun was shining so bright. But where were all the airman/people? It seemed deserted we couldn't figure out where all the 2,000 people were.

So eventually we saw some people but still not the amount of people we thought had been living there. We spoke to some of the people we ran into and then, after breakfast, we walked around and enjoyed the place. While we were there the island had a festival, so we caught a cab and went to the festival. We ate delicious food, listened to Portuguese music, and saw some performances in elaborate costumes. We stayed a long time to insure we could see it all. Then we got a cab back to the officer's quarters and ended up crashing out. My brother and I were more jet-lagged than our parents, which surprised me because my mom especially loves her sleep. My brother and I didn't wake up until 3 P.M. later that day. We stayed for only a couple of nights and then we went to Lisbon to catch a commercial plane to Frankfurt, Germany.

Germany was a familiar place to my parents because they lived there for five years when they were in the Army. They absolutely loved Germany. My Mom said my Dad wanted to retire in Germany but she said no and that she wanted to get back to the States to be with her family. When we arrived at the Frankfurt airport, we got our luggage and then went to the rental car place. Keep in mind that we didn't have any reservations for a car. However, we were blessed to get a nice BMW and we had an amazing ride.

My Dad drove us out of the airport and we were on our way. We needed a place to stay and my Dad and Mom thought we could stay at Heidelberg or Mannheim since that is where they worked and lived for many years. They were thinking it would be the perfect place because they could also show us around. But as we approached Heidelberg my Dad and Mom noticed everything looked so different. They almost didn't recognize the place. We saw an office building in Heidelberg and my Dad went in to get some information. He was told that there are no more troops located in Heidelberg or Mannheim and that all the troops and facilities for the military were now in Wiesbaden. The man gave us a number to call to see if we could get into guest housing. My Mom called and found they had rooms available. So we drove to Wiesbaden. It was a very nice place. The guesthouse was newly built and had executive suites. We got very nice suites with two rooms, a kitchen, and a bathroom. We immediately went to the commissary to purchase some food to put in the refrigerator.

Life was great! The dining facility was right next door, so we could go eat our meals or get snacks as we wanted to. We got a nap before starting to do some exploration. You see, my Dad and Mom had not been to Wiesbaden before, so it was new for them as well. We explored the post and went for evening walks. It was very quiet as well. We didn't even hear the soldiers in the morning doing their PT and singing songs. My Mom said the Army is not the Army she was in because she remembered how they use to meet in the morning to do PT and it was so motivating to sing songs and get a nice workout.

The most fun for me was in Stuttgart, Germany, where my Mom and Dad took me shopping for school clothes. It was amazing to purchase clothes from stores that at one time I only dreamed about. I remember my Dad following me around with his phone video as if I was a movie star. I know those people thought we were crazy tourists. It was so much fun. How often do young teens get to go shopping in Europe for their school clothes? I was able to buy clothes that my friends couldn't get in the United States. Yep, I knew I would be the envy of the school. We also shopped in France and England; more about that shortly.

We all had an amazing time in Germany. Although we stumbled with the German language, we did get around and saw and did everything we wanted to do. My Dad drove us around trying to find the places where he and Mom worked but as we arrived we discovered that those areas had been turned over to the German government; soldiers no longer occupied them. I know that was somewhat of a disappointment to Dad and Mom because they wanted to show us their old stooping grounds—LOL.

The plan while we were in Germany was to visit France. So my Dad talked to the manager at the Guest Quarters where we were staying in Wiesbaden and asked if we could check out of our room to go to France for a few days and then get the room back when we returned. The manager was very helpful. He said he would have a room for us when we returned but it might not be the same room. Also, he stored most of our luggage in the storage area right in the guesthouse until we returned. This way we could travel very light to France since we knew we would only be there for a couple of nights. We just took a change of clothes and our essentials.

Now we were off to another adventure. We caught the train to France and in the process learned how to figure out the European rail train system. It was a fun task, if you know what I mean. Well, we made it to France and when we got off the train the first order of business was to find a hotel for us to stay in for the next two nights. That was my brother's job since his mobile phone seemed to be the only one that had service. He was so good and fast at finding us a place to stay. All my Dad told him was to find us a place under $200 a night that was close by. My brother found us a hotel quickly and it looked and sounded good, so Dad said let's go. We flagged down a cab and the cab took us to a small quaint hotel. It was nice but it had very small rooms. It was not a room you wanted to spend a lot of time in. We only needed the room to sleep anyway. We wanted to see France, so we dropped our bags and headed out to the city to do some shopping at a nearby mall.

We went inside the Louvre Museum and saw the "Mona Lisa" and many other famous paintings. My Dad, brother, and I went to the top of the Eiffel Tower; Mom didn't want to go because she was too scared. But it was all good, and we made fun of her in a teasing manner. We traveled all over France to see as much as we could in a short timeframe. Oh, we did a lot of shopping!

So we caught the train back to Wiesbaden, Germany, and guess what? We got another room at the guesthouse that was identical to the one we had before we left. We picked up our luggage from the luggage bend and everything was in order as we left it. We were totally blessed during this trip. But that was not the end of it.

We had seen all we wanted to see in Germany and France and we were ready to go to London. We caught a commercial flight to London because we didn't want to waste any time trying to get a free flight. We were so glad to get back to an English-speaking country. It felt like we were back home. Again, my brother had to find us a place to stay and by this time he was an expert at that. He found us a nice room. While in London we visited Buckingham Place and we were able to get in because the Queen was at the Windsor Castle. While touring Buckingham Place we saw the Queen's living quarters and many other rooms in the place. It was beautiful in there. We also got to see the Queen's barns where all the horses were kept. We took pictures in the carriages and with the horses. It was so much fun. We went shopping at the famous Harrods department store in London. It was insanely amazing and it's beauty was beyond anything I have ever seen. Needless to say, that place is so expensive, but I was able to buy a few items. It was so much fun shopping there. Did I mention we went shopping?

All of us had an eventful day, and were ready to get some rest. My brother and I were on our way back to the hotel and we had to catch a train back in the evening. It was late, dark, a little chilly, and the air was breezy. As we entered the train station, we told ourselves we would read the signs very clearly to make sure we would get on the right train. Reminding you, this was one of our first nights in London. The four of us stuck together but we couldn't clearly understand all the signs, so my brother and I hopped on a train. Both of us thought out parents were right behind us, then we looked back to see if we were all on. We noticed they weren't with us, and then the doors shut. Other people on the train looked at us, some laughed, or had a serious face, but my brother and I burst out laughing because we had no idea what we just did. I was nervous, but I knew my brother was there to protect me, and I knew he wasn't that dumb. We both read the stops clearly, and got off at the correct stop, and waited for our parents. Later, we ended up meeting up with them, and we all laughed because we knew something like this would only happen to our family.

After London we all decided it was time to go home. We had come to the end of our adventure. Now to figure out if we were going to try military airlift from Mildenhall air base or go commercial. So my brother decided he would find us tickets back to Washington, D.C. He did find us tickets, but we had a long layover in Iceland. When he gave us the news my Mom popped up and said "Iceland, I would love to see Iceland." She gave my brother her credit card to book the flight. Then my brother said the Blue Lagoon is there and that maybe we could see it while we were there.

So my Mom said yes and my brother ordered four tickets to the Blue Lagoon. We got on the plane and traveled to Iceland. Iceland was by far unique, different, and the most calming place I've ever been to. I would most definitely go back to see more of it. The country is a place where you can get into a relaxation mode and let your thoughts run wild. The water at the Blue Lagoon was so warm it felt like you were in a bathtub, and when you got out it felt like 10 degrees; you would feel like jumping out of your skin. We stayed until 1:00 A.M. the next morning. Then we were on our way to the airport.

At the airport people were sleeping on top of each other, and every time we'd try to get some sleep, the cold air came in hitting our faces. Every time I thought I could fall asleep, the door would open a gust of wind would hit me. It felt like a bunch of ice cubes thrown at my face.

The entire trip was so memorable, but most of all we had each other. We planned as we traveled, we took our time, we were carefree, and we enjoyed ourselves. We had been to many places in the past but we never had an adventure such as this. We had time to really share and enjoy our time together. It was so good to get away—and to get away from our normal everyday routines. I know we're very fortunate and that we were able to experience many more things than other people. Our family is incredibly blessed with what we were able to experience.

We ended up learning different ways of living in other countries. I especially learned something new everyday. Also, you don't need to go on crazy trips like we did, but doing something that your family enjoys doing is just perfect and heartwarming. If it's hard to come up with ideas, look some up; they aren't costly, but outside of travel expenses spending time with loved ones is free. I always get stuck in the moment, and still to this day have to remind myself that I only have one family. Spending time with your loved ones is important; they could be here today, and gone tomorrow.

We may take that for granted at times, but deep down inside we shouldn't. You may never get another chance. So if you're reading this and you're thinking about planning a fun idea/trip, go for it. Grab your loved ones, and collaborate your plan, and don't regret it, even if you think it sounds cheesy. The last thing you want to say is, "Man I wish I would have spent more time with my loved ones." I don't want you to say, "I wish." I want you to think back and say, "I did." I did spend time with them, enjoyed it, took it all in, and saw how much of a blessing it is to have loved ones in your life.

It amazes me how much my family does for me, work their butts off to provide for my brother and I. So spending time with our family is the least we can do. I believe spending time with your family is priceless, and comes from the heart. I have been to many countries, and states with my family and I plan to go to a few more with them. I love going on adventures, and exploring this beautiful earth we live on. I think sometimes we don't take in and see the beautiful, amazing world we live in.

My family is a well-rounded family with lots of experiences. Both of my parents were in the military, and currently my brother is in the military as well. We love sports and are very athletic, if I say so myself. We're not your average family; we can be very interesting, some may say. We like to always think outside the box and be different from others. All of us try to encourage others on new goals and current goals. We're very rich—not money rich but loving and caring rich. We all have such a good bond, and our love for each other is strong. We're not the perfect family, but news flash: no family is.

We have our challenges, weaknesses, and hard days, but we learn from those days. We bounce back up, take our time, and learn from our mistakes. We're very collaborative and share ideas with each other. Life is too short to hold yourself back from experiencing new things. You shouldn't always experience life by yourself. Try new things with family and friends. Something sweet and cool and fun to do is making homemade ice cream (I also made some healthy breakfast cookies and they are incredibly tasty, if I may say so myself). Your family is so beyond important. They will always be your number one best friend and will be there when you feel weak. Just now, I'm realizing that when you have stepped back from most things, your family will always be there. They are truly with you through thick and thin. You can always count on them to help you pick yourself back up.

My immediate family has always been close. We joke around, we're a little carefree, and like to have fun. Growing up with them was a sometimes hard because they would pick on each other and joked around, but that's how they live in the moment, and I definitely had to adjust to that. I started to understand that they were only having fun. I was, and still am a tad bit sensitive, so it's somewhat easy to get to me if it doesn't sit right with me at first.

In conclusion for now, we love to put a smile on each other faces. We always know we can count on each other to be there when we have fallen or if we're feeling a little gloomy. If there's one thing we all mostly have in common it would mostly be our work ethic. When we have our mind set on a goal we get after it—and achieve it. It may be hard on the way, but we know we have each other to encourage one another. Here's a quote that I love, by John Wooden: "The most important thing in the world is family and love." It sounds so simple, but means so much. Cherish your time with your loved ones, always. Never take anything for granted. My father says our family motto is "God first, family second, and everything else is negotiable." Perfect!

What's Next for Gabriella?

I am sure I will write another book. I may eventually become a publisher for teens and young adults. That is what my Dad is hoping I do. But for now, I just truly enjoy hanging out with my Mom and Dad. They both are really cool. Mom loves to make me laugh and she really enjoys shopping like I do. My Dad, well, he is Dad. Awesome!

Maybe I will start a podcast to talk about my books and about other things that are going on in the world, like the Pandemic, Black Lives Matter (racism), Religion, and other stuff.

And yes, I'm planning to attend college. I'm not sure what I want to major in or what school I would like to attend. What I do know is that I'm going to college and that I'm going to have a career.

That's it! I don't have much more to say at this time. Remember, I'm only 15 years old and I'm an author. Wow, that's exciting!

Visit my website: www.gabriellamariabarner.com

Email: gabriellamariabarner@gmail.com

Word of Mouth Matters - Your Help Matters

I need your help in spreading the word to everyone you know and to everyone you don't know. Here are some ideas on how you can help get the word out to your circle of friends about my new book.

Talk about *The Getaway* by using email, or on Twitter, Instagram, Facebook, YouTube, Messenger, and blogs. Host discussions at forums where you visit as well as other places where you engage other people on the Internet. I'm not asking you to post advertisements, simply share your thoughts on how *The Getaway* made you feel and remember to share the link so they can order a copy.

If you own a small business please consider putting a display of this book on your counter to resell to customers. We offer discounts for resale for orders of 10 or more copies.

If you have a website, blog, YouTube channel, etc., please consider sharing *The Getaway* and tell them how it impacted your life.

Write a book review and publish it in your local newspaper, magazine, or website. Contact your local radio, podcast, or TV station to have the author on their show.

Give *The Getaway* as a gift for birthdays, Christmas, anniversaries, fundraisers, giveaways, and other events where gifts and prizes are expected.

Make recommendations to community groups, church groups, book clubs, and others to have the author as their guest speaker at your conventions, seminars, expos, festivals, and other gatherings.

Use *The Getaway* for small group discussions at your local church and book clubs. The author would be honored to make a surprise appearance. In short, if you help me; I am sure someone if not myself, will help you too. Thank you in advance for supporting me!!

Share my website and email with everyone:
www.gabriellamariabarner.com
email: gabriellamariabarner@gmail.com

Follow Gabby on Social Media

At the moment, I am on social media. I like to keep my instagram priviate for my family and friends. You can follow my twitter if you like. Maybe in the future I'll open my instagram to the public so be on the look out.

My parents don't want me spending time watching how other people live. They want me to create an amazing life so that people will follow me and watch my life. Sounds pretty cool to me.

Twitter: @gabriella_barn

Website: www.gabriellamariabarner.com

email: gabriellamariabarner@gmail.com

Made in USA - North Chelmsford, MA
1212882_9781952321047
12.14.2020 1701